North Sea Drama in 2 Books

North Sea Drama in 2 Books

The sinking of the Mizpah and Sail with Jim

James G Whitelaw

Swackie Ltd

CONTENTS

Book One	1
The Sinking of the Mizpah	2
Acknowledgments	3
Part 1	4
Introduction	5
1 Who Are The Swackies?	8
2 The Swackie Boats	16
Part 2	27
3 A Typical Week	28
4 The Sinking of the Mizpah	37
5 Eyewitness Account from the Mizpah Deck	48
6 Bags of Dogs	51
7 Broken Wheelhouse Windows	55

CONTENTS

8	The Fishermen's Strike	58
9	Injuries	63
10	Conclusion	67

Book Two 69

Sail with Jim – The Dream 70

Part one – The first 50 years 71

11	The First Sail	72
12	Cementing the Future	80
13	Background	85

Part Two – Lady Too 88

14	Searching for the boat	89
15	Bringing her home	91
16	Summer 2009	98
17	Summer 2010	99
18	Summer 2011	101
19	April 2012 Banff to Inverness	109
20	Through the Caledonian Canal	116

CONTENTS

21 | Corpach to Barcaldine, Loch Creran 121

22 | Barcaldine to Loch Liurbost, Isle of Lewis 123

Part Three – Punto di Svolta 135

23 | The Educated Search 136

24 | The Purchase and Planning 139

25 | Felixstowe to Scarborough 145

26 | Scarborough to Peterhead 154

27 | Winter's work 157

Part Four – A look ahead to Sail with Jim 2013 160

28 | 2021 161

Book One

The Sinking of the Mizpah

The sinking of the
The Mizpah

And other harrowing tales from fishing with the

Swackies

By

James G Whitelaw

Acknowledgments

A special thanks to **John Louie Mitchell**
for background family information
and for proof reading this part of
book before publication.

Also, a special thanks to **Jim Johnston**
for recollecting the day
the Mizpah sank. Also, for his kind
permission to publish his story.

An exceptional thanks to
Jim Bowie, the hero of
the day, without six men
may not have survived.

Part 1

Introduction

I grew up in the fishing community of Macduff, a small village with a population of only four thousand, on the Moray Firth coastline of Nort-east Scotland, where the vast proportion of boys left school and went to the fishing. That's not to say everyone enjoyed the life; it was a very tough life, away from your family much of the time.

I think it is fair to say that there were three categories of fishermen. The first group loved it and couldn't wait to leave school and get away to sea. While at school, they were, on the whole, never much interested in lessons and would gaze out the window dreaming of the day they would be free. They loved navigation class, and in art class, all they drew were pictures of boats.

At the weekends, early mornings, or evenings, they were to be found hanging around the harbour and often attached themselves to a favourite boat. They would watch for their favourite boat coming in and rush to the harbour to help them land their catch, wash down, clean and repair their gear, and get involved in anything they could.

Occasionally, a boat might have to make a short trip. Perhaps around the bay to have her compass adjusted or to move to a different port. This was an opportunity for these eager lads to get out on the water and the highlight of their year. Many of these guys chose to go to sea every time there was a school holiday from as young as 12 years old.

You were much more likely to belong to this category of boys if your family owned a fishing boat, especially if your father skippered one of the boats.

The second group of boys were ordinary boys who grew up and saw the fishing as an available job when they left school. The fishing employed large numbers of people in those days and paid better money than working ashore. Most of your mates were going to the fishing, and you could see the difference between those who went to the fishing and those who didn't. The young fishermen had big flashy cars and plenty of money to flash around at the weekend, but the guys working ashore were much more on a budget and had an old beat-up motor.

This was the largest group of boys who simply fell into the way of life and liked the benefits. They accepted that perhaps it wasn't the best life, but the compensation made the difference to them, allowing them to establish themselves on life's ladder comfortably. As they grew, they had funds and did not have to stop and consider whether they could afford to get married, start a family, buy a house, go on foreign holidays and a hundred other small things. In general, the compensation made up for the hard life.

The third group of boys, to which I belonged, weren't much interested in going to the fishing but were forced into it by lack of alternatives. It might not be that no other job was available, but that no other decent-paying job was available.

When I left school, I initially worked as a trainee storeman at Borough Briggs Motors in Elgin, where my parents stayed. At the end of every week, I got my pay packet with £14.10 inside, and it was a struggle to make it last until the end of the following week. I liked the job well enough, but when I saw my cousin, Robert, who was around the same age as me, coming home every week with over £100 in his pocket, it was a strong pull in that direction.

However, I was still cautious and decided to take one week's holiday to go to sea on my uncle's boat and see what the job was like. When you went to sea on that basis, nobody woke you in the morning. Instead, you got up when you wakened and helped around the deck as you could. Probably, I didn't get a complete and accurate picture of the job that week, but when, at the end of the week, my uncle gave me a pay packet with £60 in it, my fate was sealed, and I decided to quit my job ashore and go to the fishing.

Of course, when you think about skippers, there are fishermen, and there are good fishermen. The trick was to get a good berth, stick with it, and watch the cash roll in. That did not work well for me in the first year, as a good berth was not easy to get if you had no experience.

I landed the first berth aboard the Remembrance with Dodie Mackie as skipper. The mate was Banffie from Macduff. His proper name was William (Bill) Thompson, I think. Banffie had been a skipper with his own boat before and had quite a lot of local knowledge and was an excellent help to Dodie, a first-time skipper.

I was on the Remembrance for six months and certainly didn't make big money there. Many weeks we did not catch enough to cover our expenses and only got a 'sub', which had to be paid back later when we caught more. But, of more importance, in six months, I didn't learn very much at all and was still not an experienced fisherman who other skippers would be glad to have as a crew member.

After I left the Remembrance, I jumped around from boat to boat for a while, covering for men who were off, but in that position, you get tolerated, not learnt, so I still did not prosper much in learning the job. Then, in late summer 1977, Duthie Geddes was taking three months off from my uncle Robert's boat, the Mizpah, to go and sit his 'mate's ticket', so I got my first break and a three-month guarantee of work.

On the Mizpah, they still looked at me as a temporary position, so they did not push me, which I probably needed. After the three months, I had made good money, even on my 'half share', and learned a little, but I was by no means a proper fisherman.

A few weeks later, my grandfather told me that my uncle John would take on an extra man after the new year and that I could start there on a half-share. This was to be my first real berth, which would make me a real fisherman. The crew were my Uncle John, as skipper, the Mate and driver(engineer), his brother-in-law, Joe Watt, Old Johnny Raffan, Colin Chinchen, Stanley Ross, the skipper's son, James, my cousin and me.

Stanley took it upon himself to take me to task every time I failed to meet the standard, which was quite a lot. Stanley gave me a tough time, and I can honestly say for a while, I hated him. Processing the catch and gutting the fish was a long, laborious job, and speed was everything. I was slow, and Stanley constantly harassed me on this point. Everyone had to work flat out all the time, or the next lot of fish would be up before we had the decks cleared.

After around five months, Stanley was needling me one day. I have to admit, I had probably been daydreaming a little and wasn't going flat out, so he was right to do so. However, I flipped and challenged him to a competition to see who could gut fastest. We both started with an empty basket and as the other crew cheered, we worked flat out to fill our basket.

Some of the other crew started throwing some extra fish into my basket, but I stopped them and was adamant that all the hassle would stop this time. So finally, our baskets came up evenly and were filled simultaneously. I had made my point and proved myself, and from that day on, Stanley never troubled me again, and indeed, we became best of pals.

I have to admit, even as I became proficient as a fisherman, I never really liked the job, and as time passed, I hated it and began to think about how I could escape this life. Many fishermen who weren't committed thought like this and eventually followed other careers.

My uncle John's youngest son started life as a fisherman with his father before returning to school and graduating as an accountant. He carved a very successful career for himself in the financial sector. I have never discussed it with Paul, but I am sure he would say that the hard work and discipline he learned at the fishing was a good learning curve which has helped in many other industries.

That's probably enough of an introduction, so let's take a quick look at who the Swackies were.

1

Who Are The Swackies?

Swackie was a byname to a family who went by the actual name of Mitchell. In my earlier days, if you mentioned Swackies to anyone connected with the fishing between Aberdeen and Inverness, they knew exactly who you were talking about. More locally, it didn't have to be a fishing connection; everyone knew them. They were famous, although it may be more proper to term them as infamous.

Going back further than I can remember, there were stories which recall fights on the piers between the brothers. They were a fiery bunch, and although they fought among themselves on many occasions, if any outsider were brave enough to stand against them, they would unite as one to face a common enemy.

The Swackies originated in Lossiemouth, and a story handed down tells of a Spanish ship which went aground off Lossie and a survivor, who could speak no English, could only utter the words 'Michel', which we can assume was his name. The locals called him Mitchell, so the line of the Lossie Mitchells began.

I am not sure when they were first called Swackies, but the name is recognized in Lossie too, so it was before they came further down the coast to live. The term Swack means quick and agile, and it is thought that is why the family got the name.

My great-grandfather was born in Lossiemouth, but the family moved to Whitehills when he was young. He married Louisa Lovie, and they had three children.

The eldest child was my grandfather, James George Mitchell, commonly known in Macduff as 'Auld Swackie'. The next child was Mary Bella, who we always simply called 'Aunty'. The third and final child was John Mitchell, known locally as 'Mitchell'.

The Macduff Swackies were the family descended from James George Mitchell, and the Whitehills Swackies descended from 'Mitchell'. I am sure the Whitehills Swackies have plenty of stories, but in this book, I will concentrate on the Macduff branch of the Swackies, as that is where I have an eyewitness account of the stories I will tell you. However, John Louie, son of Mitchell, has books full of records and stories, so I hope this encourages him to collate and publish his memoirs.

First, in passing, let me give you a summary of the Whitehills Swackies. I hope the Whitehills side of the family will forgive me if I get any of their details wrong, but I will try my best to give you a summary. Mitchell married Dinah and had two sons, Eric and John Louie. Mitchell skippered the Beryl, which he later handed down to John Louie.

Eric got his own boat, first the Onward and later the Bon Accord. He later built a new boat, the Bon Ami, and Oliver McKay took over as skipper of the Bon Accord. The two boats fished together, often working on the west coast of Scotland, out of Kinlochbervie. On the last trip before Christmas 1985, tragedy struck with the vessel hitting the rocks on the dangerous entrance to Loch Inchard. The entire crew of six perished, including the skipper, Eric.

The only positive was that Eric's son, Colin, was on the Bon Accord, not with his father on the Bon Ami. Colin, however, had to watch helplessly as the Bon Ami foundered along with his father and five other very good friends. In the next chapter, I cover the vessels owned by the Swackies in more detail.

Before I move on to the Macduff Swackies, let me point out something more interesting. You may have noted that my great-grandmother was called Louisa, and Mitchell's son was called John Louie. My mother, when I come to it, you will discover she was also called Louisa. Why was this name so prevalent in the family?

Louisa Lovie's mother, my great-great-grandmother, was Betsy Gatt from Pennan, and a story has been handed down from this side of the family which answers this question. During the Napoleonic wars, Betsy Gatt's grandfather went to fight in France. When the fighting was finished, he returned to his life as a fisherman in Pennan. He never spoke much about his time in France, which was common in soldiers returning from a bloody war.

One day, sometime later, the men were mending nets on the harbourside when one of the men remarked that a strange woman and a child were coming down the brae. Betsy Gatt's grandfather looked up and said, " That will be my wife, Louisa".

The men were shocked as this was the first anyone knew he had married while in France. However, no one was more shocked than his existing wife in Pennan. He had committed Bigamy.

The French name has endured in the family since that time, but apart from my sister, Mary Louise, I know of no other in the newer generations with the name.

My grandfather James George Mitchell was born on the 21st of August 1909, a date I always remember, as I was born on his fiftieth birthday, hence I was named after him. He married Mary Hay from Sandend (Sanyne) and had five children. My mother, Louisa (commonly called Louise), was the oldest and was followed by John, Shiela, James(Jim) and Robert(Rab).

I remember my old great-grandfather as an older man sitting in an armchair and my great-grandmother as a cheery, white-haired older woman. To us, they were simply 'Didda and Ma' I don't recall Didda working, as he would have been retired when I remember him, but he also was a fisherman.

My memories of my grandfather are much stronger as he only died in 1980 when I was twenty-one years old. He was a real character who thought outside the box. He was a very go-ahead individual who never laid down the batten until the day he died. I was very young when I remember him having a heart attack, and he never went back to the fishing after that. He was pretty high-strung and could not do anything in half measures, so it mattered little whether he worked at sea or ashore; it would have carried the same stress for him.

I think he formulated a plan to set up their own fish-selling business for their own two boats, as they were currently paying another agent 5% of their catch for this service. I remember his first office, a green garden shed on a waste piece of land near the harbour. My mother and Aunt Sheila helped him with the admin parts, as this would not have been his strong point. Later, he moved to an old house on Crook O' Ness street and converted it into an office.

One day my grandmother was sitting in her chair by the window when an oil tanker drew up at her door. She watched with interest, assuming someone had come to top up her heating tank. She got the shock of her life when my grandfather jumped out of the tanker. She scolded him, 'you don't have a licence to drive a tanker'. He replied that when he got his licence, at that time, they did not distinguish between types of vehicles, and they were simply issued a licence to drive any type of vehicle. He used to proudly tell me, 'I can drive anything apart from a Sherman tank'.

Like the fish selling, he figured there were savings to be made by supplying their own fuel. After this, he also bought 'Kinghorn's garage' in Whitehills. I remember Robert and I got the job of pumping out a contaminated underground diesel tank with a hand pump. Later he set up a fish processing business at the Bankhead in Macduff.

In addition to these ventures, many other men owe their first opportunity to become a skipper to his help and assistance, both financially and practically. Quite a few men have told me that, although they did not need financial help, he had made clear to them that it was available if required.

My mother was the oldest in the family, and she went to Glasgow to train as a cook. While she was in Glasgow, she met my father, a motor mechanic in Kirkintilloch. They settled in Kirkintilloch, but after my father served his three years of national service in the RAF, my grandfather persuaded him to come north and go to the fishing, doubling as the driver, a term given to the crew member designated as the engineer.

My father went to the fishing in 1956, when the Golden Bells was new and served aboard the Bells until the Mizpah was built. He joined the Mizpah, but one year later, he decided to leave the fishing and seek a new career in the local health board.

One day while beginning a tow, one of the crew forgot to latch the roller on the stern of the boat. As a result, when the vessel rolled, one of the ropes jumped out, knocking my father, Jim Johnstone and Mikey Clark over the side into the water.

It was a relatively calm day, and the men managed to get back on board quickly enough, which was fortunate for my father, considering he never learned to swim. However, although retrieved safely, I believe my father took a different view of the fishing after that, which eventually led to his decision to change career.

My father went on to have a very successful career in the health service, rising to District Administrator and running ten hospitals around the Elgin area. Meanwhile, after raising us kids, my mother returned to school meals service, serving as head cook in Macduff Transition, Banff Academy and Milnes High in Fochabers, amongst other places.

John was the family's eldest son and took command of his first fishing boat at only twenty-one years of age. John was a massive man at six foot three inches tall, and when having a boat built, he always requested an extra big bunk for himself. Unfortunately, wheelhouses were always a standard six feet in height, so John always had to stoop down at work. So when he ordered the Dioscuri, he ordered a bespoke wheelhouse with an extra six inches of height. This is why the Dioscuri looked different from all other boats built at the time.

John was probably the most successful of the brothers, perhaps because he was the longest at the job. He finally retired and handed the Auriga over to his son James in 1985 after having successfully skippered four vessels over thirty years.

Sheila was the middle child, and where my mother was the one who would do the cooking, Sheila was the one who had to tidy up behind her. Sheila was very organised and needed to be to run the business side of her husband's marine engineering business, which flourished in the seventies and eighties. Sheila married James (Jimmy) Joiner, an engineer at Watties, the forerunner to Macduff shipyards. Jimmy set up on his own in the early seventies, also assured of the trade from the family boats.

The second youngest son was Jim, the thinking member of the family. Jim had to take over the Golden Bells when his father had a heart attack, but he also took over the burgeoning shore-based business when the old man began to falter and needed help. Jim was responsible for expanding, developing and modernising the shore-based business before, in turn, handing the business on to his son Robert.

Last but not least was Robert, often known as Rab. Rab was the wild one and always game for a laugh and fun. Rab lived life to the full but didn't look after himself. Although the youngest, he was the family's first to die, barely turning sixty. Rab was easygoing and, for the most part, simply went along with whatever John and Jim decreed was the best path. Rab always took the path of least resistance. His easy manner belied the idea that he hung on to John's coattails. Rab was an able and astute fisherman. When the fishing changed dramatically, he successfully embraced the twin rig trawling, quickly adapting and largely outfishing similar boats.

To summarize, the Swackies were great fishermen, head and shoulders above most other fishermen, but take them away from the sea and plant them in another business, and they don't outperform as they did at sea. So I think it is fair to say that they were risk takers, which worked well enough at the fishing but doesn't work so well in other businesses. I certainly know this from my own bitter experiences in other businesses.

The only member of the family I can think of who has been very successful outside the fishing is my cousin Paul who has served as financial director and managing director for several medium to large local companies. I can only assume that Paul has more 'Watt' blood running through him than Mitchell blood.

Here is the genealogy of the Macduff Swackies:
Father: James George Mitchell, born in 1909
Mother: Mary Hay, born in 1910
Children:
Louisa Mitchell was born in 1933
married James McGowan Whitelaw, born in 1932 in Kirkintilloch
Alan James Whitelaw was born in 1956
Mary Louisa Whitelaw was born in 1957
James George Whitelaw was born in 1959
(By the way, that's Me)
Jenifer Ann Whitelaw was born in 1966
John Hay Mitchell was born in 1934
married Margaret Watt, born in 1934
James Vivienne Mitchell, born in 1958, died in 2010
John Hay Mitchell was born in 1961 (Twin)
Philip Watt Mitchell was born in 1961 (Twin)
Paul Hay Mitchell was born in 1970
Sheila Mitchell was born in 1936
married James McCallum Joiner(Jimmy Joiner) born 1934
Beryl Joiner was born in 1964
James (Jim) Mitchell was born in 1938
married Margaret Briggs from Middlesborough
Robert Mitchell was born in 1959
Heather Mitchell was born in 1961
Pamela Mitchell was born in 1967
Robert Mitchell was born in 1944

married Sarah (Sadie) Johnston from Portsoy
Carol Ann Mitchell was born in 1964
Ernest James Mitchell was born in 1965
Gary Mitchell was born in 1971
Second marriage to Anne Stuart, born in 1963
Further children to this marriage

Apologies if I got any of the above wrong. My memory is still quite good, but definitely past its best.

Well, that is a more comprehensive picture of the Swackies than I originally intended to depict. We are, of course, in this book especially interested in the fishing activities of the Swackies, so in the next chapter, we will look at the long line of boats owned by the Swackies.

2

The Swackie Boats

<u>The First Beryl – BF357</u>

If we travel into the distant past, I heard the name of a boat being talked about by my mother and my grandfather. The name of that boat was the "Pansy", although I am not sure who owned it. I think it was further back on the Lovie side of the family.

The first boat I could establish coming into ownership of the family was an old small boat they bought from Wick called "Beryl". My great-grandfather and his two sons went to Wick and brought the boat back to Whitehills. This would have been shortly after the conclusion of WW2.

In those early days, we begin to see the emergence of the reckless streak which was necessary to be very successful at the fishing. One day, while fishing in Pennan bay, inside the legal three-mile zone, a local salmon coble approached them to try and find out who they were and report them to the authorities. This would have caused them tremendous problems, so they turned a hose on the small coble, drowning their engine.

The three men recovered their fishing gear and sailed away east until out of sight of the coble and men from Pennan. They then turned offshore until out of sight of land before turning west. When they were far to the west, they turned back to Whitehills, appearing to be coming from the western fishing grounds.

On arriving at Whitehills, the police met them and accused them of fishing in Pennan bay, which they denied, pointing out that everyone had just seen them arrive from the west. This cunning attitude was to remain with the family for a few generations and will show up again in my stories later in the book.

The Second Beryl – BF106

In 1947, after a few prosperous years, the family decided to buy a newer and larger boat. It was also renamed Beryl and was registered BF106 and the boat which set the family on its feet and cemented their reputation as good fishermen. They were doing very well in the second Beryl when a different type of trouble caused a family rift.

My grandfather, James George Mitchell, became a Christian and was disappointed when his younger brother, John, would not follow him down this path. The difference grew to a point where it was decided that the two brothers must split up.

Growing up, there was always a distance between the two sides of the family. There was no fighting, just a cool, distant feeling. I never understood it at the time, but it all stemmed from the point where the two brothers parted company.

The Faithful – BF205

In 1949, James George decided to buy another boat, the Faithful. Unfortunately, tragedy struck in the first few weeks James George owned the boat. The powerful Kelvin 66 engine smashed up, and the boat was inoperable.

Never ones to let the grass grow under their feet, John, in the Beryl, took the Faithful under tow the same day to the Firth of Forth, where she entered the Forth-Clyde Canal and proceeded to the Kelvin works in Glasgow to be re-engined. She was back fishing within two weeks and, for the next seven years, proved to be a profitable investment for James George and his sons, who were now leaving school and entering the family business.

The Golden Bells – BF130

In 1956, James George took delivery of a brand new boat built by John Watt and Sons, Banff. The fifty-six foot Golden Bells was considerably larger and more powerful than the Faithful, with her one hundred and fifty horsepower Gardiner engine.

Twenty-one-year-old John, the son of James George, took over the Faithful, and the Macduff family successfully continued to fish the two boats.

As my grandfather later related, during this period, he achieved a significant dream of having one thousand pounds in his bank. One thousand pounds was an enormous amount of money in those days, which was a considerable achievement. However, he used to tell me that the first thousand was the most difficult.

The Faithful Again – BF267

John continued to fish well in the old Faithful and proved to be a chip off the old block. As he gained experience and spare funds and the boat grew weary, John planned to upgrade his command. John Watt and sons were consulted again, resulting in a replacement boat being built in the Banff yard in 1962.

When she was nearing completion, the yard manager asked John what he would call her, to which John replied, we have been very successful on the last boat, so we will call her "Faithful" again. But, unfortunately, the yard manager did not have the same understanding, and when the nameplates were carved, painted and fitted, they proudly displayed her name as "Faithful Again".

The Third Beryl – BF440

Meanwhile, in Whitehills, John had continued to successfully fish the second Beryl, which was by now a weary twenty-something-year-old vessel. However, as other skippers upgraded their boats, John struggled to keep up with the new catching power and decided he could no longer delay making a further investment.

In 1966, the third Beryl was launched and proved a wise investment for John and his sons, who were now following him into the industry.

However, the day she was launched was tinged with sadness, as my great-grandmother, John's mother, passed away on the same day.

The "Bells" changing hands

James George suffered a heart attack around this time, and The Golden Bells, usually referred to as "the Bells", passed to second son Jim to skipper. Jim was assisted by his youngest brother Robert (Rab), who was in his early twenties.

The Mizpah – BF57

The ageing Golden Bells was still performing well when Jim decided it was time to upgrade. The family went to "Tappies" in Buckie (Thompsons) for their new boat this time. I remember this time well, as Robert and I, at nine years old, accompanied my grandfather every Tuesday night to Buckie to inspect the progress.

I always thought the shipyard workers said, "Oh no! Here he comes again; look busy". He must have been a real pain to them, thoroughly inspecting the building of the hull and demanding progress. We enjoyed the outings, though, as we always got Cullen ice cream on the way home.

Before coming home, though, we constantly scoured the harbour area for any Mitchells fish boxes, and it didn't matter how dirty or smelly they were; they went into the boot or even the back seat of the top-of-the-range Ford Granada, much to my granny's annoyance.

I remember the launch of the Mizpah in August 1969, followed by a great feed in the St Andrews Hotel, Buckpool. It was the following year before the Mizpah was ready for sea, but when Jim took command, the Golden Bells once more changed hands, coming under the command of my uncle Robert.

The Mizpah was a much more powerful vessel, a better equipped and finished boat and was equipped with a 320 horsepower Kelvin engine. Her abilities were making brother John think again about his command.

The Dioscuri – BF151

John decided to retain the services of John Watt and sons, who now had a yard in Macduff to build a replacement vessel. People would often inquire where the strange name came from, but John chose it with a few special personal meanings to his family.

Dioscuri was the boat on which the Apostle Paul sailed from Malta to Rome. The Greek name represented the twin Gods, Castor and Pollux, and John having twins in his family, thought this entirely appropriate.

On delivery of the Dioscuri in 1972, George Runcie took over as skipper of the Faithful Again, operating very successfully until he was eventually able to build his new vessel, the Ocean Challenge. After that, the Faithful Again was passed on to Michael Wiseman, even though, by this point, she was old and tired.

It should be noted that the Macduff and Whitehills branch of the family often helped to give budding skippers the opportunity to get a start in the industry by passing on their older vessels to younger eager proteges.

When I attended the launch of the Dioscuri in 1972 at the tender age of twelve, little did I think that I would be one of the crew only seven years later. A great feast followed the launch in Banff's now-defunct Fife Arms Hotel.

My great-grandfather must have been very proud of what his sons and grandsons had achieved. But unfortunately, this was the last launch he attended, and he was very frail at this point, unable to stand for the ceremony.

Mizpah changes hands

In 1973, the Mizpah suffered a tragic accident and a crew member, George Wood, was pulled overboard while shooting the gear. The loss of a man affected Jim quite severely, and he never really recovered from this loss. At the same time, James George was becoming less able to manage the business ashore, and it was decided that Jim would come ashore and look after the shore-based business, and Robert would take over the Mizpah, as the "Bells" was no longer fit for purpose.

Then sinks

Robert took over the Mizpah in 1974 and continued to have great success in her for a further four years. As previously mentioned, I had three months aboard her in late 1977 before becoming a permanent crew member on the Dioscuri.

In November 1978, during one of the worst days I ever witnessed at sea, the Mizpah suffered fatal damage and sank, miraculously, without loss of life. This incident will be covered in detail in a following chapter.

Be Ready – BF337

My uncles knew nothing else apart from the fishing, so had to shrug off the loss and go in search of another boat. A new boat, at least one year away, was not an option, so a search for a second-hand boat was commenced, and the Be Ready was deemed to fit the bill. Only two months after losing the Mizpah, the crew were back at sea on the Be Ready as though nothing had changed.

Robert was to fish the Be Ready for the next 16 years, first as a seine net rig, then as a twin rig prawn trawler as the industry changed. Not only did his two boys end up at sea with their father, but even Carol, his daughter, had a spell as a fisherwoman, much to the crew's consternation.

The Auriga – BF474

Although only eight years old, the Dioscuri had been pushed hard and showed signs of wear and tear. Perhaps that is putting it mildly. When we used to go to the toilet below on a poor night, when the boat gave a big roll, you got a shower with seawater pouring in through the planks. She had served her purpose, and perhaps the sinking of the Mizpah had convinced John that he needed something more substantial.

The Dioscuri was placed on the market towards the end of 1981 and sold quickly to Ireland. John could not see a suitable replacement immediately and hired a boat called the Dauntless to keep us all in a job. She was built as a pelagic boat, so it was very different from what we were used to. The engine was up forward instead of the usual midships, and the aft cabin, where we slept, was uncannily quiet.

We only had the Dauntless for six weeks when John found a suitable boat for sale in the 'South Firth'. The Firth of Forth was always referred to as the 'South Firth', as opposed to our Northern Firth, the Moray Firth.

The Auriga was a strong, able, double-planked vessel with many modern facilities, built in the Eyemouth yard. She had rope reels which were hugely labour-saving, and she even had a proper toilet and shower. We were never used to such luxuries. She also had a mess deck, so you did not have to go below to eat meals. I stayed on the Auriga until I finally left the fishing in 1985.

What's happening in Whitehills, though?

While much was happening in Macduff during the seventies, we have missed the developments in Whitehills. 'Mitchell' continued to be successful with the Beryl and was joined by his two sons, Eric and John Louie. Eric was very ambitious and also, I gather, a little impatient. Eric needed his own vessel and bought the Onward in 1974. The Onward was then sold to MDM fishselling, who eventually put Morrison Ewen in as skipper, and Eric bought the Bon Accord.

Eric fished the Bon Accord successfully and built a replacement, the Bon Ami, in 1979. Like his cousins in Macduff, he retained the older boat, and Oliver McKay became the skipper of the Bon Accord.

The Fourth Beryl – BF411

The Whitehills side of the family looked after their boats better, and they lasted much longer. Even so, at fifteen years old, it was time to upgrade the Beryl to a more modern, efficient vessel. Mitchell finally retired in 1975 and left the Beryl in the hands of John Louie, who had the task of launching and commissioning the fourth Beryl, a modern and capable boat, in 1981.

Mamre Oaks – BF57

My Cousin Robert, not to be confused with Uncle Robert, was a bit like Eric, ambitious and impatient and wanted his own command. He found a hull of a burnt-out Swedish boat in Fraserburgh and bought the boat, and restored it. He set sail after rebuilding the boat in 1983 and emulated the same success his father and uncles enjoyed.

Robert was young, ambitious and determined to be the best. He worked his men hard, but they had good rewards. He pushed everything very hard and perhaps was not the easiest skipper with which to sail.

The Ultimate Tragedy

Fishing is a challenging game, a dangerous job, and I have known many men who lost their lives at sea and boats that simply disappeared and were never heard of again. Tragedy like this stalked the fishing communities, but it was mostly a little removed from you until it struck home to your own family.

When the Mizpah sank, we were fortunate that all the men could get off. Of course, a boat can be replaced, but fathers, sons and husbands are much more precious and priceless.

On the 20th of December 1985, the Bon Ami and the Bon Accord were returning to port at Kinlochbervie. It was the last trip of the year, and everyone was genuinely excited to be going home for Christmas and New Year. Eric was very familiar with these waters, and although it was a tricky entrance, he had navigated it many times.

I do not know what went wrong, but the Bon Ami struck the rocks at the entrance to Loch Inchard, and the weather made it very difficult for any other boats to reach them and offer assistance. There were six crew onboard, and when the vessel broke up, all six lost their lives on the rocky shoreline.

The crew were:
Eric Mitchell (Skipper), 38
John Sim, 26
Matthew McFarlane, 38
David Lovie, 32
Christopher Hunt, 16
Chris McInnes, 38

The Bon Accord, other vessels, and local coastguards watched helplessly as the vessel broke up and sank. One of the observers on the Bon Accord was Skipper Eric's young son, Colin.

The one that got away.

I came ashore to work and set up my own business in 1985, but it didn't work out for me, and I returned to the fishing in 1990 before securing work in the offshore oil industry at the end of 1992. I worked mainly as a relief crew across many twin-rig prawn boats during those two years.

I had become great friends with David West, a successful skipper of his second twin-rig prawn trawler, and he encouraged me to buy my first fishing boat, offering every practical help to get me established.

Along with Alastair Mair, we scraped together a quarter of the required cash, and my uncle and aunt, Jimmy and Sheila Joiner agreed to come up with a further quarter to meet the bank's requirement of half of the price of the boat before they would fund the other half.

Jimmy was keen that we buy the Suilven, which was coming up for sale and which he already knew and maintained. We were so close to purchasing when I was offered my first job offshore.

My life changed direction suddenly in those few weeks, or who knows what would have happened. If we had bought that boat, we would have been committed to a life at sea, and it is unlikely I would ever have gone offshore subsequently.

The Mizpah – BF777

Robert had fished well with the Mamre Oaks and had his eye on a replacement vessel. Having success with rebuilding the Mamre Oaks, once again, Robert opted to buy a hull and have her kitted out to his design. He found a hull built in Sweden and had her towed to Buckie to be fitted out by Herd and McKenzie's yard.

Compared to the small wooden boats we were used to, this steel hull was massive and designed to fish in the wild Atlantic waters all year round. She was a 25m long, 250T stern trawler when completed and worked the deep Atlantic waters west of Shetland, crew changing from Scrabster.

Robert was very successful with her initially, but the Atlantic fishery changed and began to come with many more regulatory restrictions, forcing the Mizpah further afield to find the fish required to cover the hefty expenses this big boat required.

Robert eventually sold the boat in the early 2000s to a new owner in Fraserburgh.

The Fifth Beryl – BF411

In 1995 John Louie decided to upgrade again, retaining the name that had become well-known throughout the local fishing community. The fishing industry was going through many changes at this time, and smaller, older boats were at risk of being left behind. Therefore, if you wanted to continue in the industry and secure the future for your family, upgrades were becoming more critical and regular.

John Louie's son, "Bussy", attended college and obtained his skipper's certification during the next few years, and John Louie encouraged him to learn the skipper's job and take over the boat.

John Louie then formed a partnership with John Watt from Macduff Shipyards to train young skippers, continuing a family tradition of helping budding skippers get a foot on the ladder.

The Sonia Jane – BF31

By this time, I had left the fishing for the offshore industry, and my memory of some of these events is a little hazy, so I hope the reader will forgive me if I get some of the details and dates wrong.

In 1999 Robert and his sons (Ernest and Gary) sold the Be Ready and replaced her with a more modern vessel, the Sonia Jane. When the boys decommissioned this boat in 2008, this represented the last of the Macduff Swackies at the fishing. The torch was then handed to the Whitehills side of the family, who still fish very successfully at the time of printing.

The Sixth Beryl – BF440

As mentioned before, upgrades were becoming more frequent in the industry. Fifty years previously, most boats fished within sight of the land, but over the years, they had to sail further and further to get decent catches.

Into the 2000s, fishing 400 miles west of mainland Scotland at Rockall was a fairly regular occurrence. However, a sturdy vessel was required to operate in these remote, dangerous and wild seas, so John Louie and the boys decided once again to upgrade their command.

The Seventh Beryl – BF440

Although John Louie was no longer going to sea, he was still heavily involved when Colin and 'Bussy' decided it was time again to upgrade in 2019. The bigger boats rarely stop now, so a rolling crew is required. Colin, Eric's son and young John, commonly known to everyone as 'Bussy', skipper the new vessel alternate weeks.

This vessel represents the only fishing boat still operating under a Swackie command. Changed days indeed from the eighties when they operated a total of six vessels between the two families. The industry has changed, and the local cultural position has changed.

Excellent money is to be made in the oil industry with much better conditions and benefits. Locals are more likely to work in the oil industry, meaning that the boats struggle for crew and have had to source crew from as far away as Africa and the Philippines. Many Filipinos work a rota of six months on / 2 months off.

Part 2

3

A Typical Week

After dinner on a Sunday, I would begin to get a strange taste in the back of my throat. Such was the dread of another week at sea that I could already start to smell and taste the boat, even though I was several miles distant from it.

It didn't take long to grow hate of the job, and the only thing which kept us there was the extremely good money involved, which was not available anywhere else at this point, to unskilled men. It allowed me, at only twenty-one years old, when I got married, to build a brand new bungalow, with one-third of it paid cash. No other job allowed that.

A typical Sunday consisted of Church in the morning followed by a traditional Sunday lunch with all the trimmings. The afternoon would be a subdued affair as setting sail again loomed before me. After Church in the early evening, it was more or less home and then changed into my fishing clothes, which certainly smelt of the boat, despite the strongest washing powder and fabric conditioner.

I would make my way to Macduff harbour slightly before 9:00 pm. The driver was already there with the engine running, as it needed a good while to heat up and settle in. It was dangerous to start an engine and leave the harbour too soon. If you start your car, take off, and breakdown 100 yards along the road, its an inconvenience, but if your boat engine stops 100 yards beyond the pier, then you risk landing on the rocks, which is fatal, so you had to ensure the engine was well settled before leaving the harbour. Once started, the engine would usually have to run continuously until you were tied up alongside three or four days later.

As the cook, I arrived slightly before the rest of the men and started stowing away our food supplies. Everything had to be jammed into the cupboards to stop it from moving around. There was nothing worse than trying to sleep when a loose tin was rolling back and forth every few seconds, clunk, clunk.

When the remainder of the men arrived, they would make the boat ready for sea, including singling up the ropes. When moored in the harbour, you would have out multiple ropes in case one of them chaffed and broke with the boat's movement. Singling up consisted of removing the extra ropes, ready to leave as soon as the skipper appeared.

In those days, Macduff harbour was bustling, and you seldom could get a pier side berth. Instead, you had to berth alongside another boat, often up to six boats off. Every harbour up and down the coast was the same, with fishing boats employing countless men.

The crew would also check that all our gear was tied down, especially if we expected rough weather, which may result in our gear being washed overboard. Another essential check was that the lids to all tanks were secure. Water in your fuel would not end well. There were also a few times when the lid to the freshwater tank was not replaced, and when we filled the kettle to make tea on Monday morning, we discovered that our entire water supply was now salt water. In these circumstances, we had to melt ice for our fresh water. It was not ideal as there was some ammonia additive in the ice, and you started to develop a sore throat after a couple of days.

The gear would also be prepared for the following day; the Dahn attached to our ropes and only needed to be unleashed and thrown overboard when we reached our fishing grounds. The minimum net mesh size was 80mm, which had recently increased from 70mm as a conservation effort to allow smaller fish to escape and breed. As we fished predominantly for smaller fish, that affected our catch considerably.

Every Sunday night, we would remove the 'show' cod-end and put on the smaller one, which was hidden down the foxhole all weekend in case any fishery officers were around. But, of course, that would not be done yet. Before we did that, we would wait until we were out of the harbour, away from prying eyes.

Last to appear on a Sunday night, at the stroke of 9:30 pm, was the skipper and his son James. Although keen when young, at this point, 'Big John' was, by now, no keener than I was. Moreover, the entire job had become a rat race with ever-increasing government involvement and overreaching bureaucracy which took the joy out of the job.

The skipper would head straight for the wheelhouse and switch on all his electronic equipment. Essential was the GPS, and before it existed, the Decca receiver, which told you your approximate position. But, of course, these had to be set up correctly and checked while you knew your exact position.

Once you were out at sea, you depended on these electronic devices for your location. If they were out, then you would be shooting your gear blind and could be caught in obstructions on the seabed which you knew were there.

A considerable part of the skipper's job was keeping his charts up to date. The charts told him what obstructions were on the seabed. If one skipper had a problem with a 'fastener', the name for something on the seabed that snagged your gear and ruined your haul, they would broadcast this throughout the fleet, allowing all skippers to update their charts.

Once all the positioning equipment was set up, next would be the communications equipment. Typically, a fishing boat would carry between four and six radios, covering all frequencies and providing redundancy in the event one should become inoperative. Most boats also had two radars, again to provide redundancy. These were crucial during periods of fog and had to be set up correctly and calibrated.

Incidentally, John was the first skipper in Macduff to fit a radar when they became available, earning him the nickname "Scanner".

Next was a complete check on your instrumentation. The skipper had to know that his engine was running well and settled in, with no alarms showing. Once completed, the skipper would switch on all his navigation lights and instruct the crew to cast off. Navigating out of the harbour can be difficult if there are many boats, and great care was required to clear the harbour into the open sea.

As you sailed down the harbour channel, the crew would look back, watch the land recede, and resign themselves to another few days of gruelling work and precious little sleep. The following eight hours, sailing to the fishing grounds may be the last decent sleep they would have until they returned home.

Before leaving home, the skipper would have spent most of his Sunday on the telephone, talking to other skippers, exchanging news and views and deciding where to head to get the best fishing this week. But, of course, part of that reasoning was determining which skipper was telling you the truth, guessing what they were not telling you and such other considerations.

If a skipper knew there was good fishing in a particular spot, they would not want other boats there, as the fish in that location was finite. Therefore, you wanted to fill your boat before other skippers figured out there was good fishing in that area.

On leaving the harbour, the skipper knew where he was going and would set a course and work out the distance and time to the location. He would then 'set the watch', with the time divided between the crew in equal proportions. Finally, he would keep the last period for himself, which allowed him to talk to other skippers on the radio, get new information and fine-tune his plan for the week.

There was always a discussion on Sunday night, "Who had the first watch on the way in?" The watch was operated on a rota so that no one pulled the bad watch every time. No one liked the second watch or the last one. If you had the second watch, it was barely worth going to bed as you would be called out again in around one hour. If you had the last watch, you called the skipper for the last hour, and it was hardly worth returning to bed.

When satisfied, the skipper would pick an exact spot to commence fishing and call the crew out around ten minutes before reaching the location. No time was to be wasted, and as soon as we reached the location, the skipper would give the signal to throw the Dhan overboard.

We operated the 'siene net' method of fishing. This entailed shooting your ropes in a triangle formation, with the net in the middle. Each side of the ropes was 12 coils long, with a coil being 100 fathoms or 600 feet. Your ropes' total length was 14,400 feet or two and three-quarter miles. Seine net ropes were stiff fibre and laced with lead to give them the weight required to keep them on the bottom. The net would have two wings with an entrance in the middle leading to the 'bag', then 'cod end'. The wings were much bigger mesh and acted as a guide to the fish to drive them towards the entrance. Once the fish entered the bag, the mesh got progressively smaller until the fish were trapped entirely with no opportunity to escape.

Once the Dhan was thrown overboard with our rope secured, the skipper would proceed at full speed, in a straight line for eight coils, before making a 120-degree turn to the left, or the port side, if you know your nautical terms. A further four coils would take you to the end of the first side of the ropes, and we would slow down to shoot the net, a more critical time. Once the net was in the water, the skipper increased speed again and ran another four coils before making another 120-degree turn. As the last of the ropes ran overside, you should be coming back towards your Dhan. The last side of the rope was already connected to the winch, so now we would retrieve our Dhan and connect the first side of the ropes to the winch.

Once connected to the winch, we would commence winding in the ropes slowly while the boat towed the entire rig through the water slowly. As we towed, the ropes, initially forming a 120-degree angle, would slowly close over the next hour. Once the ropes were together, we would switch the winch to fast gear and retrieve the net as fast as possible. Everything was always done at top speed, as more hauls meant more fish and money.

When all the ropes were retrieved, we would transfer the 'sweeps' (wire ropes attached to both the top and bottom of the net) to the hydraulic power block. We would then haul the sweeps, then the net aboard until we came to the cod end where the fish were. The cod-end was then pulled around the side of the boat and hoisted aboard. Once inboard, the rope securing the cod end was released, letting the fish drop into the designated area of the boat.

Other boats watched and listened carefully to how long it took you to haul your net. After getting the fish onboard, the skipper reported his catch to the fleet. Skippers, however, were notable liars and would under-report so that you would not come and crowd the area where the good fishing was. Other skippers would carefully note how long you took to haul your net, indicating how good a haul was. They figured they could not trust you to tell the truth.

As soon as the last fish was aboard, bearing in mind that it may need a number of lifts if you had a good haul, the skipper was concerned with getting the boat to the next location as soon as possible. While he was doing this, the crew were getting the gear ready again. The rope man was forward, tying on the Dhan, ready to shoot. At times he barely got time to do this before it was time to throw it overboard again. The entire haul took around two hours to complete.

Another two or three men were getting the net ready, which would take a little longer. This was not a problem, however, as there were 12 coils to run before the net, leaving them plenty of time to get the net ready for shooting. Of course, this is assuming the net is not damaged. If the net was damaged, then it had to be repaired. If it was severely damaged, then it had to be pulled aside and the spare net run. The net would then be repaired during the next haul, perhaps a few hauls or even overnight. Only on severe damage, we had to wait and take the net onto the pier and spread it out at the end of the week.

When a net got worn, it was replaced with a new net and moved to the spare net box. The spare net was stowed on the wheelhouse roof as a final backup. The previous backup would be sent to the skip.

When everything was ready and we had reached the following shooting location, the entire process would start all over again, and this would be repeated all day, as long as there was daylight. This method of fishing generally only worked in daylight, so we would stop for the night and set the watch again.

This was great in the winter, as you could only get four or five hauls in during daylight. Although we always caught more per haul and worked late into the night clearing the fish, we would still get a decent sleep. However, the summer was the time we hated as we managed to push in eleven hauls a day, allowing only three hours of sleep each night. Even during those three hours, three men had to take an hour's watch each. Pity the poor guy who had the middle watch. He got only one hour in bed, called for a watch and then another hour in bed.

As the cook, during the first haul, I would prepare breakfast. Once breakfast was complete, I would prepare the dinner for later in the day, as often there was never time to do that later in the day. Apart from breakfast and dinner, we would have tea and biscuits every second haul to keep the men going through the day. In the winter, we had dinner when the day was finished, but on the long summer days, we would have dinner instead of tea, one of the hauls.

The process would start all over again early the following day, still tired. Sometimes, in the summer, after a few days, we would be so tired that as we gutted the fish, the tedious process would lull us into sleep. However, we would keep gutting fish, our bodies going through the process, even though we were fast asleep. Eventually, someone would notice and give you a shout to wake up.

We fished until the boat was full. We fished for bulk rather than quality, so we needed a full boat for a decent wage. If we had good fishing, sometimes we got home on Wednesday morning, but usually, it was Thursday morning. From spring through summer, fish were always scarce and often during this period, we often had to fish an extra day, getting home on Friday morning.

We only carried food for three days, so if we had an extra day, as the cook, I would select seven of the choicest haddocks from one of our hauls, fillet them, and they were cooked fresh from the sea. A fresh haddock like this is the one thing I do miss from my days at the fishing.

When we got back into port, everyone helped land the fish and stock up with new boxes and ice, ready for the next week. Then we all turned to our individual jobs. I had to clean the cabin, galley and mess deck. The driver had to complete maintenance and repairs on his equipment while the rest of the crew would check and repair the net and ropes.

By lunchtime, we were ready for home and would usually collapse into bed for a good few hours after a shower. The weekend was before us, and we could enjoy our efforts in whichever way we chose. All too soon, though, it was back to Sunday, and it all began again.

Of course, this was a typical week. All manner of things could turn up to upset your pattern. These included breakdowns, injuries, the need to help another boat with problems, but above all, the weather, which determined your movements and ability to fish.

The Swackies were renowned for fishing in all types of weather, and often we would be the only two boats on the sea when every other boat was tied up in port. At these times, fish on the market were scarce, and you got excellent prices, giving us some of our biggest weeks ever.

We were classed as 'share fishermen'. The total catch was sold, and the expenses were paid, including fuel, gear, food, commission, insurance, and many other items. What was left was divided equally between the boat owners and the crew. Each crew member got an equal share of the crew's allocation unless you were a young lad on a half-share.

The Swackies were always very fair with their 'square-ups', the term given to the division of the total proceeds of your catch. However, not all skippers were so fair, and many skipper's families bought their food or filled their central heating tank at the boat's expense.

This theft of money from the crew became more widespread as the years progressed and grew to proportions which could only be described as fraud. However, this general attitude of fraud and misappropriation of funds was growing in every other industry, so it should not be surprising that boat owners jumped on the bandwagon.

4

The Sinking of the Mizpah

There were very few Sunday nights when we did not set sail. The Swackies had a reputation for going out when every other boat remained tied up in the harbour. Often they were termed as 'The mad Swacks'. There were, however, some nights when things were in the balance, and Sunday the 12th of November was one of those nights.

I remember the night well, even though it is now over forty-four years in the past. We were moored at the jetty, just behind the fish market at Macduff, closest to the pier, and the Mizpah was on our off-side. All other boats in the harbour were in complete darkness. Every other skipper had already cancelled sailing.

It was one of those nights when even a wind off the land was strong enough to be singing through the rigging, and no one ventured out unless they absolutely had to. Our crew absolutely had to, as the skipper had not called to cancel, and it was, therefore, our duty to turn up.

We all went through our usual routines, although, in the back of our minds, we figured there was a better than even chance we would be going home again, even though we were sailing with the Swackies. We had all seen this before and knew the routine. The two skippers would collude and talk for a while, rubbing their hands and scratching their heads, before agreeing to hold off until they got the 'Midnight 33 forecast'.

The meteorological office issued four shipping forecasts per day, and as fishermen, we listened to every one of them by habit, even in the summertime when the weather was good. If the skipper was in bed, the watch had to listen and write down a summary for the skipper to look at when he got up.

The four forecasts were broadcast on long wave frequency 200kHz. Younger readers may have to google this to see what it means. They were broadcast at exact times. There were a few rousing patriotic tunes (Rule Britannia and such) starting at 05:45 before the first one was broadcast at exactly 05:50 each morning. The second was broadcast after the Archers at exactly 13:55 and the third at 17:55.

We were waiting for the final one of the day, which, although compiled before midnight, was not broadcast until 00:33 the following morning. It was a very familiar sequence to us, with programs for the day finishing at half past midnight; we would then hear the radio presenter say, "To take you up to the shipping forecast, here is 'Sailing by' by Ronald Binge" Sailing by was quite a pleasant tune, one which I can still hear running through my head until this day.

I have been away from fishing for a long time now, so I have absolutely no idea if this routine still continues. In the modern internet age, weather is available on demand at any time of day. Once 'Sailing By' was finished, we would hear more familiar words, "It is now Midnight thirty-three and time for the shipping forecast, issued by the Meteorological Office at twenty-three thirty on Sunday the twelfth of November one thousand, nine hundred and seventy-eight. There are warnings of gales in Viking, Forties, Cromarty, Forth, Tyne, Dogger..........Malin, Tiree, Hebrides, Fair Isle, Faroes and South-East Iceland"

Then the detailed forecast would commence, and we would pay particular attention to Cromarty and Fair Isle as these were our areas of operation. Cromarty would often be less severe as it was a more sheltered area. Fair Isle covered the area around the northern isles and was, therefore, much more exposed. I cannot remember the forecast that evening, but it would have run something like the following. "Fair Isle.

South-west severe gale nine to storm force ten, occasionally hurricane force eleven or twelve for a time".

Of course, the shipping forecast only indicated what would happen over the next twenty-four hours. The skipper would already have watched the 'Farmers weekly forecast' shown on BBC just before 1:00 pm every Sunday. He would not have been interested in the part where the forecaster told the farmers how much rain he would get, but instead would have studied closely what the isobars were showing for the week. This week's forecast had shown an enormous low approaching from the Atlantic with very closely packed isobars, indicating extreme winds.

The forecast was not good, and the general feeling was that we should go home. Rab, however, felt that forecasters were unreliable and had got it wrong too much lately. Coincidently, he had been interviewed live on TV only a couple of weeks previously, complaining that the weather forecasters were overestimating the weather. Michael Fish, a prominent BBC forecaster, was to throw this back in Rab's face only the following week after the Mizpah sank.

There was much debate for another 30 minutes until Rab got fed up and declared that he was going to sea. It was a case of 'where one goes, goes all', so we followed him out of the harbour that blustery Monday morning, heading for the 'Jungle', our favourite fishing grounds. We would return on Wednesday, but the Mizpah was never to see Macduff harbour again.

Steaming off to the grounds was easy as we ran before the wind and sea. The boat would still take some funny lurches, but on the whole, she surfed along on top of and before the waves. Only when the wave finally managed to get past us would the boat fall into a trough and wallow for a few seconds before the next wave picked us up, and we continued to surf on the crest.

We reached the fishing grounds, and it seemed like Rab had been correct. The forecasters had overestimated the force of the wind, and although quite rough, we were still able to work as usual, taking things a little slowly. We only managed five hauls that day as we were taking things easy, but also, we had good fishing, which takes each haul a little longer.

It was almost midnight before we finished processing the fish and had eaten dinner. The skipper set the watch for Six O'clock in the morning, reminding the watch to 'take the cast' at Midnight thirty-three. When we got up in the morning, it was still completely dark, but we could feel the weather had deteriorated throughout the night. The wind was howling through the rigging, and there was some debate over the VHF whether we should shoot or whether we should 'dodge' and wait.

When the weather was too bad for working, we would point the boat into the weather with only enough power to keep her head to the wind and wait until the weather subsided. But, again, Rab wasn't keen on dodging. He reasoned that we had had excellent fishing the previous day, and if we could only get in a few more hauls, then we could set sail for home that evening with an outstanding catch, which would inevitably fetch great prices when there were very few boats at sea.

Once again, Rab decided for both skippers, and we started shooting our gear very slowly and cautiously. Time was never to be wasted at this job, so it was always timed to shoot our gear and be started towing before daylight started to arrive. For some strange reason, the best hauls of the day were usually what we termed 'the making of daylight' and 'the darkening'.

The problem was that the weather and seas were often subdued in darkness and increased at daylight. This was not always the case, but it certainly was on Tuesday 14th of November, 1978, when the Mizpah had less than twenty-four hours to remain afloat. During the next hour, while we towed our gear and closed the net, the wind strengthened into the worst day I had ever seen at sea.

If you consider that I was part of a crew regarded throughout the fishing industry as madmen who went to sea in all types of weather, then perhaps you can begin to understand how bad the weather was that day. The wind was so strong that it was whipping the tips of the waves off in a horizontal spray which completely blinded us looking into the wind.

While we were towing, we had been, while not exactly into the wind, at least sheltered in part from its full force on the aft deck. Once the ropes were all in, we would tow the net to the surface, upwind, but not directly upwind, in case we drifted down on top of the net when we started to haul through the power block, when the propellor had to be shut off.

When the skipper finished towing the net up, it was a mad rush to get it into the power block before it started to go down again, and the weather started to push the boat downwind from the net. For the first part of the sweeps, we were drifting down past the net, so it was very easy, but then as we drifted past and were hanging with the net like a sea anchor, things became very difficult.

We had a very powerful hydraulic power block, but even with this power-assisted machine, we often pulled in ten feet only to watch nine feet being yanked back out again. So we had to be very careful where we stood and where we put our hands and fingers. If we were to get caught up in the net, we could be yanked out with it and suffer severe injuries or even fatal consequences.

Never were seven men so glad to see the net retrieved and the fish aboard so the skipper could point the vessel into the face of these hurricane-force winds. There was no more debate now. It was self-evident that to continue fishing was not an option. The only consideration now was what to do for the best. Do we dodge or head for home?

It was academic, as heading the boat into the wind was also the direction of home, so the only thing to decide was how much power to put on. Do we dodge at minimum power or give her a little more power to keep us moving ahead? Dodging was okay if it was for a short time, intending to recommence fishing, but with strong winds, as we had now, it was doubtful we could start fishing again that day or even the next day.

Dodging kept your head to the wind, but in reality, you could be going backwards, which with wind from the southwest, you would be going further away from home, more into the open sea with possibly stronger winds and higher seas. So we had no option but to put more power on the engine and start to edge in the direction of home and 'smaller waters'.

We were under no illusion that this would be an easy day. I can't speak for any of the other crew, but I had never seen a day like this in my few short years at sea and have never seen one since, either on a fishing boat or an oil rig.

We dodged along with every crew member squeezed into the small wheelhouse, just watching the seas coming at us. But, unfortunately, you could only see as far as the next wave crest as the water was streaming off the top, completely obscuring our vision. Then for a brief moment, we would be carried up to the top of the crest where we had a slightly more transparent and more extended vision, but one which you did not want to see as all around us were giant angry waves, crashing onto anything which got in their way.

The Mizpah was one-quarter of a mile on our starboard side, but most of the time, we could not see her. When we were down at the bottom of a trough, and the Mizpah was in the same trough, it was like looking down a long, long tunnel at a distant ship, and then she was gone again. I have never experienced that vision again at any point in my long career at sea.

Again, I can only speak for myself. I had no fear. The Dioscuri was a decent boat in which we had seen some pretty horrendous weather, even though, perhaps not as bad as this. It never occurred to me that perhaps we might be in danger. Of course, I was only nineteen years old, so maybe I was simply young and naïve.

It was 1:00 pm on Tuesday, 13th November, and although we did not yet know, the Mizpah had barely twelve hours left afloat. The VHF crackled, and Rab told us they were taking water, but this was not unduly concerning.

On the Dioscuri, we had a pump which ran almost continuously in bad weather, as the planking was not perfectly waterproof. If the pump had problems, we had a backup pump generally used for fish washing and could be rerouted to pump out the bilges.

We also had an auxiliary engine with a powerful pump that could pump out the bilges in an emergency. Often, things happened on a boat, resulting in an excess take on of water, especially in poor weather and high seas.

On the Mizpah, the driver would go below to put on more pumps, while some of the other crew would go forward and sound the spaces to see if there was a problem. No case for concern at this point. However, only fifteen minutes later, Rab contacted us and told us that the crew had reported five feet of water in the main hold.

This was very concerning as the main hold was only around ten feet high, so it was already half filled with water and had begun seeping into the engine room. The air intake for the engine was around six feet high in the engine room. If the water reached this height, the water would flood the engine, rendering the boat powerless. No power meant no ability to pump out the intake of water. Once the engine stopped, it was basically all over.

The Mizpah crew continued to investigate to see if pump intakes were blocked or if there were any other ways of pumping out the excess water. However, by two-thirty, it was apparent that they could not stem the flood of water and the coastguards were alerted, and a search and rescue helicopter was scrambled.

The crew of the Mizpah were now resigned that the boat was sinking beneath them and looked to the helicopter heading in their direction as their salvation. By this time, other vessels on the sea had also been alerted through the standard emergency channels, and some were being managed by the coastguards, standing by to offer assistance if required.

Around three-thirty in the afternoon, the helicopter arrived on location and commenced rescue operations. Before the helicopter can commence rescue operations, the first step is to establish a connection with the vessel. Once a connection is established, the helicopter can hover offset to the vessel and conduct operations without the risk of coming into contact with the vessel's mast and rigging, which could be fatal.

The helicopter passes down a thin line to the vessel with a weak link in case it gets snagged. This operation is the most dangerous as it must be done with the helicopter directly overhead the vessel. This is particularly a problem in small fishing vessels, as they have high multiple masts and superstructures spread over the entire deck. To get the line to the deck, the helicopter crew must get the messenger line down without snagging anything on the way, which is very difficult when a boat is bobbing around wildly in a hurricane force twelve.

The crew tried three times to establish a line but were unsuccessful on all three occasions. The pilot was to tell us later that while he hovered overhead, sometimes there was a seventy-foot gap, and at other times the masts almost came into contact with the helicopter. Eventually, the helicopter, having limited fuel aboard, had to give the crew of the Mizpah a distressing choice.

It was clear that the helicopter would not be able to lift the crew off the boat, so to conclude the rescue, the crew would be required to take to a liferaft where the helicopter crew knew they could reach them without obstructions in the way. I can fully understand the reluctance of the crew to board a flimsy liferaft in these mountainous seas, but what was the alternative?

While the crew considered this, the helicopter became critically low on fuel. So it departed for base to refuel, with the possibility of returning, although it would certainly be dark by the time they could return. Meanwhile, the coastguards, working in the background, had located a larger vessel in the vicinity.

Aberdeen-based Millwood had concluded a three-week trip in Icelandic waters and was heading home to land their catch on Wednesday morning. However, the coastguards diverted the vessel towards our location and were now formulating a plan for the Millwood to carry out a rescue operation.

We could not go alongside the Mizpah as wooden boats would be in danger if they came into heavy contact with each other. It could well end up with two vessels being lost instead of one, two crews being lost instead of one. A larger steel vessel provided a more viable option, which, while it could still damage the Mizpah, posed little risk to the Millwood being a far sturdier build. The Mizpah was already doomed, so the only concern was staying afloat long enough to get the crew off.

The Millwood arrived on location shortly before 6:00 pm and sailed around to size up the situation. Her master, Jim Bowie, consulted with Rab and John about how best to proceed. It was decided that we would go upwind and stand by to spread some oil onto the sea. Have you ever heard the term 'spreading oil on troubled waters'? There is a reason for this saying. In difficult seas, a thin layer of oil prevents the waves from breaking and briefly calms the sea.

Calming the seas was to be our contribution and hopefully enough to allow the Millwood long enough to go alongside the Mizpah and get the men off. So, while we moved some of our barrels of engine oil from our engine room up to the deck, the Millwood, aware that the Mizpah could sink at any moment, started to get into position on the windward side of the Mizpah. This was the safe side as they would not want the Mizpah drifting down on top of them.

We emptied four five-gallon drums of thick engine oil overboard. When the oil spread down to the area of the Mizpah, the Millwood darted in to come alongside the forward end of the Mizpah, where the deck was higher, and the Millwood would not be towering so high above the Mizpah. It was all over in seconds, and the Millwood pulled out again to avoid damage.

Then the news was handed down to us that only four of the crew had managed to get off, and there was still a further two onboard the stricken vessel. So the Millwood would have it all to do again to attempt to rescue the remaining crew members. Fortunately, Skipper Bowie was calm and level-headed and wasted no time in moving back alongside and almost before we knew it, the entire Mizpah crew had been plucked to safety.

As the Millwood continued her journey towards Aberdeen, the coastguards stood down all parties on standby as the crisis was over. However, as we watched the Millwood disappear to the south, our skipper, John, had other concerns on his mind. As far as the coastguards were concerned, the operation was complete, but John had a financial stake in the Mizpah and had begun to assess what that meant for him.

It is amazing! You think you are the only two boats on the sea, but other vessels appear out of nowhere when something happens. Firstly, a salvage tug, the 'Yorkshireman', appeared on the scene, and John was starting to think about what kind of claim would arise if the tug were able to salvage the Mizpah.

Around 6 pm, when the crew were rescued, the wind was howling, but two hours later, the wind had died completely down to zero. We must have been in the eye of the storm, and the sea had dramatically subsided. John thought this was his opportunity to do something and hatched a plan to take the Mizpah under tow by the stern and tow her to Wick, which was only some thirty miles distant.

Two hours after the crew were plucked to safety, we were bumping alongside the Mizpah, stern to stern, with John issuing instructions for his son James to jump aboard and secure a rope. James refused to board a sinking vessel, and we pulled off again. John had planned to take her in tow and have a man standing by with an axe to cut the rope if she suddenly sank. I think it was a scary idea and probably was well, we did not carry out this plan.

We stood by the Mizpah, unsure about what to do next, when another boat appeared on the scene. You may remember, at the beginning of the book, I outlined the origins of the Swackies and told you about my grandfather, James George and his brother John. I didn't say much about his sister as she didn't figure in the fishing narrative. Not only was she a woman, but also, her family were all girls.

However, Mary Bella's oldest daughter married a Portsoy man called George Sutherland, known locally by the bye-name 'Hatties'. This same George Sutherland appeared in his boat, the appropriate named 'Sans Peur', a French name with the literal translation, Without Fear.

Four boats floated around, and nobody was sure what to do. So we hung around and discussed a few ideas until past midnight, and then John thought it best we get some sleep and we would see what transpired in the morning. So we climbed into our bunks at 1:00 am, and I remember Stanley saying, "don't get too comfy; you will be up within thirty minutes to try something else.

You got used to instantly following asleep at sea, so it was a rude awakening for me when the buzzer, which usually woke us, sounded. I looked at the clock, and it was 1:20 am. I had been asleep for only twenty minutes. The chatter was, "George has launched a raft and is going to put a rope on the Mizpah".

We staggered up the hatch, bleary-eyed and to our amazement, there were two men in a liferaft just leaving the Sans Peur, paddling towards the Mizpah, pulling a rope behind them. They were halfway across when the Mizpah suddenly tipped over on her side, hung there for half a minute before upending with only the forward end of the boat showing, then finally slipping below the water at 01:25 am on Wednesday, 15th November 1978. I often wondered what would have happened had those men been five minutes earlier in going across to the Mizpah.

5

Eyewitness Account from the Mizpah Deck

The following Is an eyewitness account directly from Jim Johnston, who was the chief mate on the Mizpah at the time.

This is a memory that I will never forget and will live with me forever. Your description of the day is perfect and describes it as it happened.

We were trying to get to the lee of land as the wind was so strong and yes you are probably right in your description of that day that it was probably one of the worst days we had experienced at sea.

We, as you said, we were all in the wheelhouse together as the weather was nothing like we had ever seen before and even since retirement of my days at sea.

We were faced with a massive wave and it was like climbing the face of a cliff but on reaching the top it was looking down the other side of a cliff and when the boat hit the bottom of the cliff, so to speak, the boat felt as though we had hit a brick wall and it was a shudder that scared us all.

I went to check the engine room after this and could see water pouring through the Fish room bulkhead.

I immediately went back to wheelhouse and suggested to Rab to slow down so we could check out the fish room.

Dodging slow into the wind we discovered on opening the fish room hatches that the fish room was well full of water with boxes floating back and forth in the fish room.

I noticed on the deck beside the winch that deck planks had sprung and assumed that this is where the water was pouring into the fish room from the deck.

I imagined also that if deck planks had sprung that it was possible that some of the hull planks had also sprung open due to the force of the boat falling head first into a hole in the sea after falling over the wall or cliff of sea head first .

It was definitely the case that hull planks had sprung because there was not a chance that deck planks sprung would have taken so much water in such a short time.,

The picture still in my mind was we were looking down into a hole in the sea and it was like falling headfirst off a cliff face.

As you would imagine a freak wave would describe it.

As we look back now, we would consider ourselves very lucky to survive this ordeal.

What troubled me more than anything was the fact that Mikey Clark & Robert Junior were unable to get off her at first attempt from Jim Bowie of Millwood.

Because of the strength of wind, we were screaming at them both to jump when the boats came together.

Mikey had bad eyesight and his specs were covered in spray and he shouted I can't jump because I can't see.

We threw a rope to Mike and shouted to tie this rope around his waist and to leave at least 3/4 fathoms behind him and tie the tail of the rope to Robert Jun because we could see he was in shock and he said he couldn't do it, he couldn't jump because he was in shock.

Next time Jim Bowie came against the Mizpah we could see that the top rails from the deck upwards had broken away and it was clear that the Mizpah was going down for sure.

We screamed at Mikey right we said when we say jump you must jump.

We had all the Millwood crew on the foredeck to help and when Mikey grabbed the rail, we found strength from somewhere to whip him on board the Millwood.

Because of the swell the two boats drifted apart and with a result the rope attached to Mikey came tight and pulled Robert junior into the water.

Unaware of this to skipper Jim Bowie he knew we needed another man and God knows where our strength came from, but we pulled that rope so fast that Robert was up at the Millwood rail in seconds and we just had Roberts legs in over when the boats came crashing together again.

Two seconds more and Roberts legs would have been crushed.

I am not a church going man Jim, but the good lord was definitely with us on that day.

It was not funny but looking back on the time to jump, when we all left the galley to go out into the freezing cold the last thing Mikey said to Skipper Rab was should I switch off the gas hobs on the cooker.

This was our only source of heat after we lost engine power.

By this time the water was level with the top of the main engine.

Someone once told me that if that had been a steel boat she would have gone down before water reaching that level.

That was a day never forgotten but we survived to tell.

My only disappointment of the whole ordeal was that Jim Bowie should have been given an award of courage and seamanship for saving our lives on that day.

6

Bags of Dogs

We were all very quiet, as you tended to be on a Monday morning, at the beginning of a long summer day and probably a long summer week. Anticipating the next four days with perhaps only three hours of sleep a night was not a happy prospect. Then 'Big John' popped his head out of the wheelhouse and said, "John Slater is up and down with dogs". A strange statement, perhaps, to those who have never been at sea, so I had best explain.

Whitefish were light fish, and they floated when you towed the net up. Dogfish were quite something else. They are very heavy and sink. When you tow and snag something on the bottom, one of your ropes rides higher in the water than the other because it is stretched tighter. That is the first indication you have 'taken hold of a fastener.

When you are amongst dogs, you tow as usual, but as soon as you switch to high gear, the boat goes hurtling backwards until your ropes are straight up and down, hence the expression 'up and down with dogs'.

We never fished explicitly for dogfish, but most years, they appeared some week, just out of nowhere and then in a few days, they were gone again. They always seemed to be in immense shoals, and at times, you could have a massive haul of dogs one haul, shoot right alongside the next haul and not get a single dog. By now, you will, no doubt, have figured that to us, a dog meant a dogfish, not a four-legged furry man's best friend.

The year before, we had our biggest haul ever of dogs. The Dioscuri held four hundred boxes in the hold, which we filled before beginning to stack them on the deck everywhere we could. It took us around eight hours to get them all onboard, and the boat was very low in the water when we set sail for the harbour.

Once all your ropes are in, you may remember that I said you tow the net up. That takes much longer with dogs, and the net begins to sink fast as soon as you take the power off the boat. Getting the sweeps transferred to the power block is a considerable problem, and then the block struggles to cope with the weight. Frequently the skipper needs to tow it up again while you are hauling the net. The power block is simply an aid. It does not haul the net for you.

Once you get the sweeps in and get to the toe of the net, then it becomes easier. Long practice and learning led us to fit a 'dog rope' to the net. The dog rope was seldom used and was only for occasions like this. When you got it up, you connected it to another rope to the winch. The other end of the dog rope was connected directly to the cod-end lifting strop, allowing us to winch in and lift the first lift of dogs onboard. After it was emptied into the pond, the cod-end was retied and thrown back into the water, allowed to sink and fill with dogs again before repeating the process. This continued until you had all the dogs onboard.

When we got into the harbour, we had to start by boxing all the dogs on the deck to clear our feet. It was, once again, a long, laborious process, but finally, we were all done and landed a total of seven hundred boxes exactly, a colossal landing for us.

Back to the present, though, and John announced, "George is up and down too". This was George Runcie, skipper of the Ocean Challenge. That was one boat on either side, so we waited expectantly to see if we would have dogs. When we switched to high gear, sure enough, we went headlong astern, indicating a heavy load in the net.

John tried to tow the net up, but it was not rising very much. This load seemed much heavier than we had ever seen before. We tried all sorts of things to try and get the sweeps into the power block over the following hour, but nothing we tried worked. The weight was too great. So finally, John reluctantly came up with the plan to run the net out again with one coil of ropes, then attach the end to a Dhan. We would then return and retrieve the net in a few weeks when the dogs had either escaped or rotted.

Pause for a few seconds here, consider that we managed to haul a seven hundred box load last year, and consider how big this load must have been.

We ran off the coil of rope and dhanned the net, and then began fishing again with our spare net. The next haul, we had fifteen boxes of white fish (haddock, whiting, cod, etc.) and not a single dog in sight. Other boats around us were still getting dogs, though. Our third haul, once again, we were hurtling astern when switching to fast gear. Once again, the weight was so great that we could not get the sweeps into the block.

John was adamant that he would not Dhan another net, so he hatched another idea. We would tow the net slowly to shallow waters near the harbour, then when we stopped, the net would not have far to sink, and we would manage to get the sweeps into the block and haul up the dog rope.

There was one major problem with this plan. John was not at the front of the queue the day they were dishing out patience. Slow ahead was five hundred revs on the engine, and top speed was eleven hundred and fifty revs. John kept adding another fifty revs until we ran at one thousand revs.

When we got to the harbour, John briefed us, "get everything ready, and when I stop the boat, haul as fast as you can". When we hauled, it was effortless. Only the headrope of the next was left. The rest had broken away in the last sixty miles, probably quite near the beginning.

That, however, is not the end of the story. Remember the net that we Dhanned? We still had to retrieve that net. Three weeks later, John decided that the net had been there long enough, and we should go and try to haul it. We winched in the ropes, and they came quickly enough. There certainly was no significant weight there now.

However, before we got all the ropes up, the net started to come up with them, all twisted around the ropes. The net had been left for twenty-one days, and we later realised that there were forty-two twists in the gear, one for every tide change during this period.

It was a nightmare for us as we could not simply reel in the ropes. We had to place a strop around the whole lot and lift it twenty feet at a time. It took us hours, but finally, we got the cod end up, and there was only one lift there, not of dogs, but of many bones with rotten flesh attached. When we lifted it onboard, some men were violently sick due to the stench.

Our whole boat was stinking, we were all stinking, and when we pulled the net up onto the pier to try and untangle it, the overpowering stench permeated throughout the entire town. Once again, the Swackies were not popular.

7

Broken Wheelhouse Windows

The Dioscuri had a strange look to her as the wheelhouse had been adapted to be high enough for John's six-foot three-inch frame. The shipyard cut off the usual wheelhouse and replaced it with a custom, higher fibreglass wheelhouse.

Instead of sharp definite corners, the corners of the wheelhouse were rounded, with the corner windows made of pliable Perspex instead of glass which would not be suitable for the curved opening.

By the time I joined the crew, these windows had seen eight years of successful service and had proved themselves a great idea, but that was about to change.

The prevailing wind in the UK is from the southwest, which means that sailing home from our fishing grounds to the northeast of Macduff was very often directly into the wind and heavy seas. In those days, boats did not have the complete protection they have now, being fully covered in and water/weatherproof. We had a whaleback and a deck shelter, but there was a gap in the middle which was open to the weather, and this area contained the hatch to the fish hold.

In poor weather, heavy seas would come aboard and flood the area and could also find their way down into the fish hold, having to be pumped out. If we were working, the skipper had to keep the engine speed down to try and minimize the amount of water coming onboard.

He did not want to do this as he wanted to get ashore as soon as possible and get his fish landed.

I am not sure if big John would have worried about us getting soaked or having more difficulty working, but the threat of water penetration forced him to ease the throttle in a little until we finished working the fish.

On our last night, on the way ashore, we would be working the fish, and when we got to the last of them, I would go aft and get the dinner going. Usually, I would go aft, switch everything on, and then come back on deck. Once we got to the tidying up stage, I would go aft, take off my gear, check on everything, lay the table and many other things.

On a poor night, we would try to keep things simple, so no fancy pudding on this night; I would merely mix up some Angel Delight and open some cans of fruit to compliment the roast beef dinner. Dinner was well advanced, and I went down into the cabin to mix up the Angel Delight. As I started this, with it in a large bowl, whisking it by hand, I could hear the guys up above come in and start to take their gear off.

Some were in the galley, at deck level, but others were in the engine room, hanging their wet things up to dry by the engine's heat. I heard the skipper ask if everybody was off the deck, and then when he got an affirmative, he put the throttle full down. The boat had not even reached full speed when suddenly the entire vessel shuddered, hit by a massive wave, which engulfed the entire boat.

There was an almighty crash, and water started pouring everywhere. The corner window had broken, and water flooded into the wheelhouse with such force and quantity that it continued through into the galley and down the trap into the lower hull. At the same time, the partition between the wheelhouse and the engine room had many apertures for controls and instrumentation, so the water also flooded through them into the engine room.

I was in the cabin, mixing up the Angel Delight, which suddenly lifted out of the bowl and ended up all over the wall. I looked out the cabin door, which was latched open and was horrified to see the water cascade down the open hatch.

I watched as the engine room door opened, and Dodd Slater, who was covering for someone who was off, tried to escape the water coming into the engine room. He opened the engine room door to get out, but when he saw the quantity of water coming down the trap, he ran back in and closed the door again.

There was brief pandemonium, which probably only lasted for around five seconds before the skipper pulled the throttle back and turned the boat away from the weather. I think I was the only person on the boat who stayed dry, as the cabin was the only place that avoided the water. Even though they were soaked, the guys had to put back on their oilskins and go out and patch up the window.

The water had damaged our electrics with radios, radars, GPS, lights, and automatic pilot all ruined. Every electronic piece of equipment in the wheelhouse was utterly swamped and out of action. Being in the wheelhouse, Big John bore the brunt of it and was literally soaked through and through.

As skipper, we were never accustomed to seeing him change his clothes, and we found it quite amusing to see his underwear hung up to dry. I couldn't help but think his pants were so big we could have used them for a sail.

There was a significant delay before the lads finally sat down for their evening meal. It was all part of the job, though, and we just got on with it. When we got home, the skipper had to organise replacement equipment for all the water-ruined electronics before Sunday night.

Three weeks later, the very same window broke again, and we had the same process to go through all over again. When we got in that weekend, John had the opening plated and welded shut. It would never happen again.

8

The Fishermen's Strike

Fishing had become problematic after the UK joined the Common Market, as the EU was known in the 1970s. Part of the agreement included the common fisheries policy, which has been hated by fishermen now for around fifty years. As a result, throughout the 1970s, fishing became increasingly tricky, and government regulation became increasingly tighter.

In 1975 there were huge blockades of all British ports, which resulted in some help from the Government, but did not address the real problem. However, the problems continued, and as the industry moved into the 1980s, unrest again reared its head, and the fishing vessels declared a blockade of Scottish ports.

On Wednesday, the 18th of February 1981, I had been sitting at home for three weeks without work and pay. The blockade did not seem to be doing any good, and the fishermen and the related shore support industry were the only people losing money. We were not affecting the Government, and they were not interested in a solution.

Early in the afternoon, the skipper called. "Be down at the boat for 9:00 pm, don't tell anyone and don't switch on any lights on the boat." There were some pretty strong views on the blockade, and there was no telling what some men would do, especially if they had just come out of the pub with a good few drinks.

It would be much easier for us to go to sea if we could go undetected. It would, however, not be simple, as the Glendeveron was tied up with multiple ropes across the harbour entrance. The crews of the Dioscuri and the Be Ready would have to help move the Glendeveron out of the way to allow us to egress from the blockaded harbour.

We worked quickly, without showing any lights, carrying out all our routine tasks simply by the streetlights around the harbour. We concentrated on the essentials and left the unnecessary until we were clear of the harbour.

The Glendeveron had been tied up across the entrance with multiple ropes and many strong points on four piers. We had to untie the Glendeveron, escape the harbour, and tie it up again while drawing as little attention to ourselves as possible.

I don't remember any trouble, but there were reports of someone trying to stop us. I do not have any recollection of that.

We worked fast, cleared the harbour and on our way to the fishing grounds reasonably fast. For us, it was simply a typical week starting, but it would be anything but a typical week.

Nobody had been on these fishing grounds for almost four weeks, so the grounds were well-rested, and fish were abundant. We had never seen such good fishing, and we filled the boat in only four hauls and were underway for Macduff harbour Wednesday evening.

Around two hours (twenty miles) from the harbour, the shore lights start to come into view. At first, it was merely a source of light and undefined, but as we came closer to the shore, it became apparent that there were much more lights on show than we usually saw. Coming closer, we could see hundreds of cars lining the Station brae and vantage points all along the shoreline.

As we came within viewing distance of the shore, we could see thousands of people lining it, and we guessed they were not in a friendly mood. It was a beautiful night, and the sea was like a millpond. It was so calm we could moor the two boats alongside in the bay. Contact was established with nominated representatives on the shore, and discussions began about what we would do next.

It was agreed that a delegation would come out from the shore and negotiate a resolution to the situation. We needed to enter the harbour and land our catch, but the fishermen who had not worked for four weeks were angry that we had broken the strike.

The Macduff harbour pilot boat came out with four local skippers onboard who were tasked to negotiate a settlement. Unfortunately, my memory is a little fuzzy now, so I cannot recall which skippers came out. I remember Bill Watt and Maurice Slater were there, but I can't remember the other two.

We were all lining the aft rail as the pilot boat came alongside, and the representatives boarded. I recall Rab standing there with a twinkle in his eye. He looked at Bill Watt and said, "Well, Bill, you are aboard. Do you think you will get off again?"

Our two skippers and the four visitors sat around the mess deck table with a cup of tea and began to hammer out a deal. We needed to land our catch, but we needed their cooperation to do this safely. They knew that, ultimately, there was no way to stop us from landing our catch, so it was a case of a little compromise on both sides

Over the next hour, an agreement was made that we would be allowed to enter the harbour and land our catch, but our fish had to be sold by an independent fish salesman who would collect all the proceeds, which would then be sent to charity. That may sound very straightforward to you, but the practical outworking of that agreement was a little more complicated than anticipated.

As we motored slowly down the channel, the entire shoreline was lined with an angry mob who were baying for blood, our blood. Fortunately, the police had barriered off the entire long pier and the area around the fish market. Still, to get there, we had to negotiate the channel between the long pier and the Duff Street jetty, manned by angry mobs with as many stones and other missiles as they could carry, determined to carry out their revenge on us.

As we entered the harbour, Joe Watt began to go up onto the whaleback, where we usually put out a rope to spring us around the corner. Someone asked, "Where are you going, Joe?". "To throw a rope, Joe answered. "You can't go up there, Joe. They will kill you". Already the missiles were starting to rain down on top of us, and we had to take cover.

I don't pretend to know what was going through big John's head. He knew we were in danger, so perhaps he thought he would distract the crowd for a moment, but it was as big a shock for us when John released a distress flare right into the heart of the crowd. It landed behind the crowd at the foot of Duff street, and I think he was very fortunate that no one was hurt by his actions. However, it certainly distracted the crowd for a few seconds, which was all John needed to power the boat between the two piers and safely to the fish market.

The Be Ready followed us in, but the crowd had recovered a little and pelted them with assorted missiles. They had a rougher passage than we had, but we both eventually tied up alongside the fish market and began to land our catch. During the landing, the angry crowd continued to assault us with the only thing left to them, verbal abuse and insults.

It was a small town, and everyone knew everyone else, where they lived, what family they had, what type of car they drove and much more. I remember one angry protestor who was more vocal than all the rest, or perhaps just louder. Robbie Annan had been screaming abuse for two hours solid.

"Scanner", he howled, "you used to own a Mercedes, but it is a burnt-out shell now". Quick as a flash, John shouted back, "No problem, I have a new one on order". This type of abuse continued for the entire three hours it took us to land our catch and restock for the next week. Then we had to think about getting home. I can honestly say that it is the only time in my entire life I have been in the back of a black Mariah. Finally, the police obliged us with a run home.

Of course, the story doesn't end there. The fish had still to be sold, and the money sent to charity. Well, it didn't quite work out that way, either. It had been agreed that Alastair Paterson would sell the fish, and our guys went along with that. However, Jim carefully noted who bought what fish during the sale and tallied what each fish merchant had bought.

We were the leading supplier to most of these fish merchants, and it was reasonably simple for Jim to ring around them and tell them that they would get no more fish from us if they did not settle up directly to our office. Ultimately, we got paid, and no money was sent to any charity. The strike was broken, and most other skippers were too busy planning to return to sea to take much notice of this small item. And so the blockade of 1981 was ended by the Swackies.

The flare had landed near the Moray bar at the bottom of Duff street, and the woman who owned it, egged on by angry fishermen, pressed charges against big John. The case came to the Sherriff's court in May, and the Sherriff admonished John, which caused another minor uproar amongst local fishermen, and calls of corruption.

The entire episode was then consigned to history to such a degree that I could not find any reference to it, though I searched diligently online with many different search terms.

9

Injuries

It has always been recognized that fishing is a dangerous job. I have already detailed tragedies where men have lost their lives, and entire communities are tipped into mourning. Yet, I have barely scratched the surface of all the heartache dished out to fishing communities around our coast.

Quite apart from the ultimate tragedies, there were also many day-to-day injuries and wounds suffered regularly. However, we accepted it merely as part of the job and got on with things as best as we could. I suffered a few injuries myself in my time, and although trivial, worth listing to give the reader an idea of what fishermen face daily to bring fish to your table.

On one occasion, I jumped down from the aft net box and must have landed wrongly. I went over the side of my foot, and pain immediately shot up my leg, which went from under me. I could put no weight on my foot and was convinced I had broken my ankle. There is not much you can do with it in the middle of the ocean, so I struggled as best as possible. Fortunately, there were no broken bones, and it healed gradually, although my ankle was weak for months afterwards.

We were well used to a rolling boat, and our bodies automatically moved with the deck, compensating for the vessel's movement. However, at times, a rogue wave would hit the boat with such force that the vessel would move unpredictably and cause us to reach out to brace ourselves.

On one such occasion, I found myself away from anything to grab onto and was hurtled towards the other crew who were gutting at the rail. Automatically, my arm and hand went to the rail to brace myself as I flew towards it, and I managed to hold myself against the ship rail.

Colin Chinchen had been gutting there, and as he grabbed support, his knife pointed upwards. When we recovered, he indicated his knife and said, "You were very lucky there". I pulled off my glove, showed him where the blood was dripping from my wrist, and replied, "perhaps not so lucky".

The blade had gone straight in, and although it was pretty deep, it was a straight clean cut which caused me no lasting problem. Forty years later, I can only notice the mark because I know where to look for it. I was, indeed, lucky.

I had a previous chapter on dogfish. They came with their own set of problems, not least of which was the vicious spike that they had behind their top fin. Often they came in such quantities that we merely threw them forward, then down the hold in large heaps. With so many dogs flying around, catching a spike was always a danger for which you had to watch out.

On one haul, a spike caught me on my upper thigh and tore a piece out of my leg. The spike itself didn't do much damage, but the wound got infected and bothered me for the best part of a year afterwards.

Once while hauling our net through the power block, a loose rope with a shackle fell from the block and hit me square on the mouth. It made a mess of my face, but the worst of it was internal. I just felt the teeth in my mouth disintegrate and felt like I had a mouth full of sand. Several visits to Albert Robertson, the local Dentist, resulted in several crowns to replace my broken teeth.

Knocks, bumps, scrapes, cuts and such were so common that most are not remembered. I was fortunate that these were the worst I suffered, or perhaps I was simply more alert to danger and quicker to avoid it.

However, it was more than just yourself. We were a steady crew, had been together for quite some time, knew each other and watched out for each other. That had a big part in the fact that I only ever witnessed one serious accident at sea.

Like all accidents, when everything is going well, then nothing happens. However, it adds to the risk when out of the everyday routine things happen. For example, the weather was always a present danger and risk we faced, and as mentioned before, we regularly went to sea in poor weather.

On one such day, a moderate force eight gale had given rise to strong seas and sizeable waves. We had seen much worse, and we had no particular concerns. Our ropes were all in, and we were towing the net up, and old Johnny Raffan complacently had one of his hands resting on the ropes. A particularly big wave went through, which caused Johnny to grip the rope for support. At the same time, the rope wraxed out through the steel roller and took Johnny's hand with it.

Johnny was in great pain and went into the galley while we hauled the net. It is the most dangerous time of the haul when you have a net near your propellor, so nobody could be spared to help him until the net was onboard. After the net was hauled, James, who had done some first aid, went to Johnny's aid, examined the damage and helped him bandage his hand up.

Johnny had two fingers amputated, and the rest of his hand was in a mess. So we hove to for a while. James worked with Johnny, and John radioed details to others around us. After a while, John looked out and asked Johnny, "Are you OK?" Fishermen are not ones to admit weakness and always play down any pain or injuries, so through gritted teeth; Johnny replied, "Y.y.yes, I,i,i'm OK".

With a cheerful voice, John replied, "that's good. We will just continue to work away then". James was very unhappy with his father as he knew how bad the injury was. It was almost two days later before Johnny had his wounds attended to in a hospital. After that, he never returned to the fishing again.

As previously mentioned, we were fortunate to have had little to no injuries onboard. Unfortunately, most other boats did not fare so well, and chapters could be written detailing the many injuries suffered in the industry. However, this is not the subject of this book, so we will leave others to tell of these things. Conclusion

10

Conclusion

Those stories are from the late 1970s and the early 1980s, forty years ago. What has happened since then to the guys mentioned? Sadly I am the only remaining member of the crew of the Dioscuri from those days. I was the youngest, but still, too many of them were taken before their time.

The first to go was big John, then Joe Watt. James suffered a heart attack and died at only fifty-two years old. Although the oldest in the crew, Johnny was a tough old horse and outlasted three of them. Colin Chinchen died five years ago, and Stanley Ross followed only two years ago.

When Stanley died, this spurred me to tell these stories. I figured they would be lost forever once I was gone, just as that way of life is now. However, fishing is an entirely different ball game now. It is no longer a cottage industry but a complex, high-cost industry where only a few fishing families have survived.

The Swackies in Whitehills continue to have a fishing boat, with two of Mitchell's grandsons skippering the vessel on alternate weeks. But, of course, there is also much to take care of ashore these days, and John Louie and his wife Mary are still involved in helping out ashore, whether it is getting in the stores, picking up and dropping off crew, or a thousand other requirements.

In Macduff, most of the family have moved on, with most of them involved in the oil industry, either offshore or onshore support. The entire area has changed. In the 1970s, the fishing industry employed thousands of men along the coast. Now only a handful of men in this area are engaged in fishing, with the oil industry becoming the principal employer.

However, the sea is in our blood, and many of the men, once involved in the fishing, have taken up careers in the marine industry, either on rigs, supply vessels, standby vessels or many of the marine support services required by the oil industry.

A few have even embraced the sea as a hobby or pastime, with many owning small creel boats, which the local harbours now rely on to fill their berths. Personally, I had had enough of fish but still loved the sea. So I opted to buy a small sailing vessel and the second book will tell you of some of my adventures which arose from that passion.

Book Two

Sail with Jim – The Dream

Sail with Jim – The Dream
by James G Whitelaw
Copyright James G Whitelaw 2021

I dedicate this book to Albert Robertson and my Uncle Jim, who first introduced me to sailing.

As a young lad of only ten years old, Jim Whitelaw is taken sailing with a friend of the family. Jim is totally enthralled and from that day forward Jim decides that one day he will buy his own yacht. It is forty years later before Jim eventually keeps his promise to himself and this book reflects the story and steep learning curve during Jim's forty-year journey. Jim buys his first boat without too much knowledge and makes many mistakes and gets into quite a few scrapes. This book follows Jim's dream and nightmares.

Part one – The first 50 years

11

The First Sail

I am not sure how old I was. Certainly it was a very long time ago from my now 61 years old. It must have been around 50 years ago, probably around 1970 or thereabouts.

Early on a fine summer's Saturday morning, Albert Robertson, a close family friend, and also the highly esteemed and very well respected local dentist arrived to pick up my cousin Robert and myself to go sailing on his small yacht which he kept in Gamrie harbour. We were going to sail the yacht from Gamrie up to Banff.

Gamrie is the local name for a village in the north-east of Scotland which has the real name of Gardenstown. The village was founded by the local superior, Alexander Garden of Troup in 1720, and is today regarded as one of the major influences in the UK fishing industry.

Albert owned a holiday cottage in the neighbouring, but smaller village of Crovie, and berthed his yacht in Gamrie harbour during the summer. I don't know which model of yacht the "Kittiwake" was, but I do remember it very clearly and estimate it at around 17 feet long. It had a drop keel and an outboard engine if I remember correctly, but things are starting to get a little fuzzy now. I suspect it was a Leisure 17 or similar type of yacht.

It was all white with a small porthole window forward in the cabin at either side. Whoever had painted on the name, you didn't get computer generated vinyl graphics in those days, had made a very good job of it, and on each side, up forward on the hull, not only was the name prominent, but it was proceeded with a very good picture of a kittiwake.

It was like going on holiday. I was so excited. I had been around boats all my life, my dad and my entire mother's family being fishermen, but this was different. This was a yacht.

Maybe these ocean going sailors would laugh at me, but if a boat had sails, to me it was, and still is, a yacht, regardless of size, and yachts were exciting in a way which fishing boats were not. There was something about going through the sea without any engine noise, peaceful and quiet, free and gliding like a bird soaring on the thermals.

This first trip kindled an interest in me which was never to be suppressed, and although it was to be another 40 years before I bought my first yacht, the deal was sealed on that day.

I am not sure how long Albert had owned the yacht, but he certainly seemed to know what he was doing and imparted some of that knowledge to our young heads, as best as he could. Albert would sit at the helm and instruct Robert and myself in handling the sails and ropes.

The "Kittiwake" was a light responsive boat which sailed well even in light winds. Around our coastline, there were thousands of Kittiwakes, a small seabird, like a miniature seagull, but cute and without the harsh predator look of the bigger bird. Albert pointed these out to us and explained where the yacht's name came from. There were literally thousands of birds which nested on the cliffs of nearby Troup head, which has since been declared a bird sanctuary.

I am sure we had some sandwiches and drinks packed somewhere in a little bag, as we were always hungry at that age, but to tell you the truth. My memories don't extend to trivial little items like that, but to the more important things.

We travelled down to Gamrie in Albert's Citroen. In those days there weren't many foreign cars on the road, not like today, so the car was a bit of a mystery too. I don't think I had experienced much beyond Ford, British Leyland and Roots cars. For young people who don't remember, Roots was the name which Chrysler had at that point.

I won't even try to explain British Leyland; you will have to Google it. It really is a different world 50 years down the road.

Arriving in Gamrie, 6-7 miles from our home in Macduff, we wound down the brae in a small village which was completely different from our home a few miles away. In fact it was so different; it could have been in a foreign country. The culture was different, life's pace was a little slower, and they even seemed to speak a different language.

Albert seemed to understand the language though, and know the locals, so perhaps we would survive. Little did I know that only about 10 years later, I would marry a young girl from this "foreign" village, and less than 20 years later, would move to stay here with my family.

Driving down the steep brae, you could see the harbour long before you reached it. It kept disappearing and re-appearing as we wound our way round the ever descending hairpin bends on "Gamrie Brae". If you are reading this book, and have never been to Gamrie, then I have to say, you have missed out on one of the most beautiful spots in Scotland. Make a plan to visit, but best do it in the summer, as it can be a very remote and bleak place in the winter, like many of Scotland's treasures.

We eventually parked up on the pier at Gamrie, and the harbour was full of little fishing boats. Most of them were small creel boats (Lobster pot boats for the English), but right there, out in the middle of the harbour was the Kittiwake. In fact, many of the boats were out in the middle of the harbour. I wondered how the owners got to them, and how we would get out to the Kittiwake.

We stood on the pier and looked out to the Kittiwake and I hoped that I didn't have to swim out to it. We did swim a lot in sea in those days, and didn't mind the cold, but I didn't have a towel with me today to dry myself, and I had no "dookers" (Swimming trunks).

Albert took off to the south pier and we toddled behind. He located a rope on the pier which he loosed out quite a bit. Back to the East pier where another rope was located and pulled in, bringing the Kittiwake right alongside a ladder so we could board her.

I was in my element. For the first time in my life, I was on-board a yacht. Young though I was, I would begin to learn a little about how a sailing boat worked, what all the ropes were for, but right now it was all a mystery.

I am sure Albert must have had some preparation to do before we were ready. There was a small red tank with fuel we had taken down with us in the car, and down the ladder. I guess that had to go somewhere. To be honest, I don't remember a whole lot. I just remember untying the Kittiwake and leaving the ropes attached to a buoy and the ladder to be retrieved later when we returned with the boat.

Actually, we never returned to the buoy. Although we did make this westward journey a number of times, we always left the boat in Banff, so I guess someone else must have sailed the boat back with him, or maybe he did it single handed, like I tend to do on most of my trips.

With the outboard engine running, we motored out of Gamrie harbour into the shelter of the "Muckle rock", which guarded the harbour entrance. We rounded the rock, and once out into "Gamrie Bay"; we got the sails up and shut off the engine. We began to move along by sail power only. I don't have a date, a time, or even a year, but this was the exact time when my love of yachts was born.

We sailed out of Gamrie Bay and out past Mhor head, one of the two mighty pillars which dominate and guard Gamrie Bay. In Gamrie bay, there is a strip, just a few miles wide, which is made up of crumbling red sandstone. This strip runs about twenty miles inland past Turriff, and you can tell where it is, as you can see the old houses made out of the red stone. At Gamrie bay, at the western side, you have Mhor Head, a craggy outcrop which separates Gamrie from Greensides, a long sweeping rocky beach. On the eastern side, you have the massive granite headland of Troup Head, which is one of the most important colonies of sea birds in the north of Scotland.

High up on Mhor there is an ancient church, "The Church of St John the Evangelist", which was built to commemorate a victory over the Vikings at the point of Mhor in the year 1004AD. The "Battle of the Bloody Pits" was a resounding victory against a foe that were pretty formidable, and the skulls of three of the Danish chieftains could be seen in an alcove in the church walls until about 1970, when the skulls were stolen. They were subsequently recovered but are now kept in Banff museum for safe keeping.

It is amazing how different places look from the sea, as opposed from the land. If you are planning a visit to Gamrie, then do try to get a trip out to sea to view the village from there. One of the local creel boats will oblige, and you could even have the opportunity to help them pull their creels. I remember my days as a fisherman and when you looked along the coastline at night, from the sea, Gamrie looked bigger than some places ten times its size, simply because it was built on a hill.

The house I have in Gamrie now is at the top of the village. It is only about ¼ mile from the harbour, but it is up at 140m, or around 450 feet in "old money". From the sea, you get an absolute spectacular view of Gamrie, the entire village. None of it is hidden. Each part is higher up than the street below, so you see it all. At night, from the sea, it looks like a city, even though there are only around 200 homes there.

I am sure Albert had sailed this route a number of times before, as he was able to keep us fairly close into land and keep the trip interesting for us. Round Mhor head, heading west, you come into "Greensides", which is a long sweeping bay, full of rocks with no possible landing place for anything other than a very knowledgeable local with a small boat. In days long ago, there was some salmon fishery carried out here and there are the remains of a salmon bothy at the far western side of the cove. There is also a very rough, steep track where some poor horse would have had to pull up a cart loaded with fish and equipment, and even their boats. The cliffs which surround Greensides are all around five hundred feet high, and any time I have been down there, I was always breathing very hard before I got back up to the top. For this very reason, it is very much an unspoilt beach.

There are a series of bays like this all along the coast, each one different and interesting, and all the way to Macduff, including one which opens up into a series of gorges containing all the water which makes its way down to the sea from the area behind all these majestic cliffs. These are known as the "burns of Cullen" locally. The furthest east we had ventured as kids was the "Salmon Howe", but our mothers didn't know that. That was the sort of place you hadn't been told so, but you just knew, you weren't allowed to go there. It was a desolate deserted cove where, if anything were to happen to you, then you could lie there a long time before you would be discovered. It was east beyond Tarlair, up over the golf course and down the other side.

We sailed past the "Salmon Howe" and into the bay at Tarlair. Now we really were into home territory. We spent most of our free time in the summer at Tarlair outdoor swimming pool, one of the finest in the country, in those days. I remember summer days with Tarlair absolutely packed with thousands of people, pipe bands playing, galas, paddle boats..........those were the days. We would spend all our free time in the summer there, and even after school went back, we would rush home from school at four o clock and be changed, a quick bite to eat and off across the golf course and climbing down the cliffs to Tarlair in as short a time as possible.

The cold never seemed to bother us much in these days, and I begin to wonder about the kids today, and even about ourselves. Is it the introduction of central heating which has made us softer? I don't really know, but right through until the pool closed at the end of September, we would be there until they shut the gates at 8:30pm every night. Our mothers never had to wonder where we were in those days.

Just off the big pool at Tarlair, there is rock, right in the middle of the small protective bay. Albert expertly took us right into the bay, inside the rock, even to 20- 30 feet from the poolside. All the Saturday bathers look at us. Nobody had ever seen a boat come in there before. Robert and I had to stand in the bow and watch out for any rocks or boulders and shout back to Albert at the helm, so that he could take evasive action.

So we negotiated our way around the rock and back out to sea, in full view of envious bathers, some of which were our friends. I was on top of the world, so proud. Every one of those young boys eyes were glued to us as we sailed in so close to them, and then sailed off again. It must have been high tide, as I have seen that whole area dry with very dangerous looking rocks many of other times.

From there we continued our way past Berryden quarry, the "Black cove" and The Black Cove was another of these places you weren't allowed to go. These were the days before environmental awareness, and this was where the town dust cart deposited its load when it was full, straight into the sea.

It really makes you wonder. We have cleaned up our act so much these past forty years, and all of a sudden there are no fish in the sea, which had thrived there for thousands of years. Could it be that we are not as smart as we think we are, and we are actually interfering with nature and changing the order of things which have gone on for centuries?

Between the Black cove and the back of the harbour at Macduff there was a rocky beach, all of which we knew intimately, having scrambled over the rocks many times, fallen in, tumbled and gained many scratches, bruises, bumps and cuts, none of which I remember or did me any harm. Well, there was the one time we got cut off by the tide. I managed to jump across and only got my legs wet, but Robert hesitated a little too long, and in the end had to strip off, throw across his clothes and swim. He was just getting dressed again when our mothers appeared on the scene searching for us. It was well past our bed time, dark and they were pretty agitated. Hey, it was all good fun, part of life's learning curve, and in the end, we are still alive, aren't we? Mothers worry too much. So do wives!!!

Continuing our sail, we had to sail out past the "Collie rocks", which are a pretty dangerous set of rocks just off Macduff, mostly submerged just out of sight unless it is a real low tide, then out across Banff bay before taking down our sails and motoring into Banff harbour and tying the Kittiwake up. Forty years later, I still remember this day, the day which introduced me to my expensive hobby. Albert, if you are reading this, my wife says you have a lot to answer for.

12

Cementing the Future

We had a number of Saturday morning sails on the Kittiwake, each one as exciting as the first, each one reinforcing the thought, "One day, I am going to own my own yacht".

Unfortunately, we all get to that age where we find ourselves in a "Saturday job". For me it was more of a case of a summer job, and since the summer was sailing time, I guess the two just didn't fit together. All summer, for around four to five years, I used to go down and work with my uncle, "Jimmy Joiner".

Joiner was his last name, but in fact, he was a marine engineer, working on the many commercial fishing boats in Macduff and Whitehills harbour and often further afield. In the summertime, they were always very busy, as boats had scheduled regular maintenance for the period when the boat was tied up to allow the crew to go on the summer holidays.

I would assist them in stripping down and overhauling the old 6 cylinder Gardiner engines and even older 3 cylinder kelvin engines, usually being assigned the mundane task of cleaning up the cylinder heads, ready for refitting. I would work eight till five, Monday to Friday, back for five-thirty to eight-thirty on Monday, Tuesday and Thursday nights, and also eight till twelve on Saturday mornings.

I could probably fill another book with stories from this period in my life. Stories like the time I fell into the harbour in Whitehills, toolbox and all. Or how about the time I dropped the big 2 metre long steel governor pushrod on Andre's head. Oh He was angry, and I didn't run fast enough. These stories are for another time.

These were long working weeks for a young kid and during this time, the carefree reminders of sailing on the wind slipped from my mind.

I am not sure how many years later, years can seem like centuries when you are a kid, so it may well have been only one year, or could have been 3 or 4. One day, I came home from school, climbing the "Meter Hill", the local name for the top part of Skene Street, Macduff, where we stayed, and here, out in front of my Uncle Jim's house, 2 doors up from us, was a yacht on a cradle.

She was a beauty. I could see right away, she was not the same as the Kittiwake. She didn't have a drop keel. She had a massive fin keel, and in her cradle, she towered over me. She was a big boat. She must have been 26-28 feet, but looked massive to me at that age.

I don't remember her ever having a name, and I am not sure that my uncle Jim owned her very long, maybe even just one season or two. I do, however, remember going sailing a few times in her, mostly at nights, after school. This would have been just a little sailing around the bay, but again, to me, very exciting.

One particular sailing trip stuck in my mind, and taught me a lot about how these boats worked. We were coming back into Macduff harbour. My Uncle Jim berthed the boat on the long pier, just ahead of the Lifeboat berth, which was the first spot you came to when you entered through between the Long pier and the Duff Street jetty.

I guess the wind was favourable, and my uncle Jim decided that we would be able to come into the harbour under sail. My cousin Robert and I were each assigned a head sail rope for tacking, and after some practice all the way in, we had it down to a fine art.

As we entered the harbour channel, and especially as we came between the long pier and the West pier, there really wasn't much room for tacking, but I remember my uncle Jim, standing at the tiller, us waiting for his command. The boat would almost be touching the pier at one side before he swung the tiller and shouted out "NOW". One of us paid out while the other hauled in as fast as any professional race crew.

That was a very exciting entrance to the harbour, and I would turn over in my head these manoeuvres, coming to an understanding of how a sailing vessel worked. We were able to take the boat right into the harbour and tie it up without the need for an engine. This was invaluable training for me, as I would have to do this later in life a number of times, through necessity.

Through my teenager years, many other things took up possession of my mind, as they do, and sailing faded a little. The fascination, however, would never completely go away, and there was always a thought in my mind, "One day, I am going to own my own yacht".

Years later, after I was married, I think, we were up in Aviemore, and I spied the sailing dinghies for hire on Loch Morlich. There was a fresh breeze coming down the loch, but I talked my wife, Pearl into it anyway, and hired a sailing dinghy for a couple of hours.

These were very light boats, not like what I had sailed in before, but I knew the principles of how they worked was just the same, and knew how to make them go. Once I got it out there, right up to the line of buoys which the owner said I wasn't allowed to go past, I got her onto a broad reach and she was flying. Of course, we had to sit right up on the windward rail, as the dinghy was keeled over to the limit.

It only took minutes before Pearl was screaming and had to be rescued by the owner in his rib and taken ashore. She probably saw her whole life flash before her eyes, and was absolutely terrified. To me, that was what sailing boats were meant to do. It was great, and for the first time in my life, I was at the helm, flying along on the wind.

I guess you could say that Pearl was never going to encourage me to get a yacht. She had had quite enough on Loch Morlich to do her a lifetime. She was, later in life, to say to me, "I will be quite happy to go in a yacht with you, if you buy one which doesn't tip over". Tall order.

The next time I was sailing was probably twenty to twenty-five years later. It was the year 2000, and we had three days down in the Florida

Keys, before going up to Orlando. Behind our hotel, there was a guy hiring Hobbie Kat catamarans. I hired the small vessel, I am not sure you could even call them a boat, for the entire day. There was a big inlet, probably around two miles across in both directions. My only restriction was I was not allowed out to the open sea.

I sailed around that inlet the whole day. Sometimes the kids would come with me, other times on my own. I did use sun cream, but you wouldn't have thought it. That night I had to go into a cold bath to try and cool my skin down. Again, though, I had a most enjoyable day, a memorable day, which stirred up the long pent up yearning inside me.

After the time in the Florida Keys, there was a definite reawakening of my interest in sailing. Many would be the time I would look out to the bay and see a sailing boat being carried along on the wind and wish I was there. I would also take time to stop and look at yachts lying in various marinas. There were some great examples on the Clyde, when we were visiting Pearl's auntie Rosaleen in Greenock.

Gamrie harbour was always full of small creel boats, but they just didn't interest me, in fact, the smell was a real turn off. For lots of guys, there dream was to have a small creel boat and to shoot a few lobster pots. I am afraid that held no interest for me, much to my Father-in-law's regret.

My father-in-law loved his creel boat, and after retiring from the fishing, due to a heart attack, he had another twenty five years in which he enjoyed his boat. He used to look half dead in the wintertime, but when summer came, he would take on a new lease of life, and the boat was dully painted, launched and the creels, which he had painstakingly repaired over the winter, were brought out.

He loved his boat so much that often he would go out on it every day in the summer, even though some days he did not feel all that well. In the past few years though, his summers were becoming shorter as life started to catch up with him. At the end, he was found round in Greensides, a creel on his knees, having suffered a massive heart attack while out on the boat. It was hard for the family, but for him, it was his life, and the way he always said he wanted to go.

I did mute the idea of a boat with a few of the harbour committee in Gamrie, and got no encouragement at all, including from my own father-in-law. They just didn't want yachts in their harbour, only creel boats. For the older guys who had grown up in the really tough years, they just could not understand why anyone would want a boat from which you could not earn some money. It was non-productive and that just did not compute with them.

Now and then there were yachts in the harbour. The Laird had one there for a while, but then they could hardly deny the Laird a berth. There was also an old beat up yacht which Glen had in the harbour, which actually sank. I think this just reinforced the idea they did not want yachts in the harbour. I think the turning point for me was when my neighbour Iain got a yacht.

Iain already had moorings in the harbour, and he simply went and bought a yacht and put it onto the moorings. The old guys in the harbour probably weren't really happy, but he got away with it, and the door was opened. That was probably the point when I made up my mind to start a serious search for a yacht. It probably tied in with the realisation that I wasn't getting any younger, and if I were to do this, then I realistically couldn't afford to wait much longer.

Around ten years previously, I had had a little spare cash and had toyed with the idea of buying a yacht. We had also visited Florida that year and I really liked Florida. It was either a yacht or a villa in Florida. Pearl didn't want either of them, but I guess the villa in Florida may have been the lesser of the two evils and she relented. The yacht was pushed back.

This time, 2007, there was to be no pushing back. I was not getting any younger. This had always been a dream, and I could not allow the idea that I would look back in twenty years' time, having missed the opportunity, and fading into old age with this regret hanging over me. I was finally going to get my own boat.

13

Background

As I write the next few chapters, there is absolutely no doubt that you are going to hear some strange tails, and observe some strange behaviour from me. I think, before we go there, it will help set the scene, if I give you some background to help you understand my thinking, sort of like trying to help you understand why I have done some of the crazy things I have done.

When I was 17, I went to the fishing to work. I can't ever say that I really liked it, but it was a job and it was really good money for a young lad. For seven years, I went to sea with my Uncle John on the Dioscuri and later on the Auriga. The "Swackies" were noted throughout the North East of Scotland for pushing it to the limit. They would go out to sea when other boats were tied up for bad weather. They would be the last boats to come back in when the weather deteriorated.

Some would say that they had no respect for the weather, but I would have to disagree. My Uncle John took the weather very seriously and never missed a shipping forecast. There was a healthy respect for the sea, but not a fear of it. He knew how far he could push it and get away with it.

He either taught me that same response to the sea or it has been passed on to me in my genes. I have a healthy respect for the sea, and have seen what it can do many times. One notable occasion was when we watched our sister ship, the "Mizpah" go down in a force 12 in

November 1978. Fortunately, this time, there was no loss of life, but as fishermen, we all knew boats and men which had simply disappeared.

Like my uncle, I respect the sea, but there is a part of me which likes to push it to the limit, and I probably do not have the same fear of the sea as some other sailors, many of which have no sea-faring background at all. Many a time in my life, I have been absolutely soaked to the skin, and to me, that is simply part of going to sea. As long as I have a dry change of clothes to change into, it is no great problem.

I am also impulsive and impatient. This in itself is going to explain a whole lot later on. If I make up my mind to do something, then I just want to get on and do it. I will speed up and gloss over preparations to get it done faster. If I decide I am sailing somewhere, then my goal is to get there as fast as possible, no leisurely cruising, sailing only a few hours every day. You can cover a lot of ground when you sail overnight.

I don't like waste. I like to get the things I want in the most efficient way, and really don't like to buy anything I will rarely use. I am, however, willing to pay more for an item which will cover more than one purpose. I am often reluctant to replace items which still have a little use left in them. I like to get good use out of every item I pay for.

If I get a "bee in my bonnet", I can suffer from tunnel vision. Sometimes I am so focussed on something, that I do not properly examine other peripheral issues.

Finally, and perhaps the most important item, I am an eternal optimist. Sometimes this is a good thing, but at other times, which I have found out to my cost, it is not very good when you just cannot see the potential downside. If you cannot envision problems, then it is difficult to properly prepare for them.

I hope that this gives you a little insight into the mind of the author and that you can subsequently figure out why I did so many crazy things as you read through the book. I'm still here, so obviously I didn't push it too far, but I would have to say, I have changed my outlook some as a result of some of the mishaps and scrapes I got into. Maybe also as I get older, I like my comforts better and I am not quite so fit and able as I used to be when I was young and lithe.

Yes, those of you know me now; I was once young and fit. When I got married, I was strong as an ox and only ten and a half stone. This overweight, underpowered and unfit man which you all know is all Pearl's fault, or so I like to tease her. Married life has done this to me.

Part Two – Lady Too

14

Searching for the boat

Summer 2007 saw me start to buy sailing magazines, searching through the "For sale" adverts and also to look longingly around marinas, paying particular attention to yachts for sale. I visited all the small harbours up and down our coast, not only looking at boats for sale, but also sizing up many of the different types of yachts available, and trying to figure out which type would be best for me.

I formulated some idea in my head of what I wanted. Firstly, a bilge, or twin keel boat would be necessary if I wanted to keep it in Gamrie harbour, as the berths all dry out at low tide. Secondly, it needed to be of a size which I could easily manage single handed, preferably around 22-28 feet long. Thirdly, it needed to have accommodation, as I wanted to sail a little further afield at times and stay on it overnight.

After looking at many different types of boats, I was very taken with the "Hunter Horizon", in particular, the 23 and 26 feet versions. I felt the 21 foot version was a little too small, and the 26 had everything I needed, so what would be the point of going any bigger. There was a nice 23 foot Horizon for sale in Findochty, the "Bramble", and I looked at it a number of times in the passing. The price the owner was asking, I felt, was a little high, so I did not take it any further.

A few years later, in a brief conversation with the owner's wife, she told me that I had almost bought their last yacht. This showed me two strange things. Firstly, I must have contacted them. I hadn't remembered that, as I had looked at so many yachts. Also I noted the term "our yacht". I just somehow couldn't imagine those words escaping from Pearl's lips. Any boat I did buy would most definitely be "his boat".

In the summer of 2008, I located a 26 foot Horizon down in Southampton and gave this very serious consideration. At £12k, it would be a large expenditure, similar to buying a car, and so I pondered over it for a while. Unfortunately, as I pondered, the biggest recession since 1929 was hitting the world, and my business was certainly not immune to it. I could see that cash was going to get tight, and decided that it would not be prudent to spend this amount of cash at the moment.

My son, Andrew, also decided that he would take an interest in sailing, and intimated that he would look with me and that we would "go halves" when we finally bought a boat. He was looking through eBay and spied a 20 feet Vivacity which was in Inverness. The advert stated that she was fully kitted out and ready to go sailing, and although she was almost 40 years old, we thought that this may be worth considering further.

The seller was asking £2,500 for the boat, and it certainly wasn't going to break the bank. We also considered that it might be good to start with a cheaper boat, learn the ropes, make any mistakes and try it out, before getting a bigger and better boat. In the end, we decided to put in a cheeky offer of £2,000 and it was accepted, to our surprise.

I guess we put the offer in, not really expecting it to be taken seriously, and it was a surprise to us too that we suddenly found ourselves the owner of a boat, not really the type which we wanted, but it was ours now, and we had to go with it. We hadn't even viewed the boat, which was lying at Muirtown marina in Inverness. So, we found ourselves on the train to Inverness, and once again, imposing on "Auntie Rosleen and Uncle Donald" for an overnight stay before sailing her home the next day.

15

Bringing her home

Pearl, my wife, dropped Andrew and me off at Keith station where we boarded a train to Inverness. Donald and Rosaleen met us at Inverness station and took us down to Muirtown to view the boat.

At this point, I think I need to say that you are going to read a fair bit about Donald and Rosaleen. Rosaleen is a sister of my wife's father, and to be honest, everyone should have an "Auntie Rosaleen". I would never manage to pay her back for all her hospitality over the years, and for all the times I have simply turned up on her doorstep. You will see what I mean later.

Lady Too lay in Muirtown marina, and was better than many of the clapped out vessels which lay there, but at only £2k, we weren't expecting too much, and we weren't disappointed. Everything was there which you needed to sail her, but it was a basic package. Of course, being our first purchase, we probably didn't quite know what to look for, so it was pretty much going to be a case of buy it, then see how it went.

She had a trailer, but we had already decided that we would rather sail her home and collect the trailer at a later date. The trailer, like the rest of the package, was a little dilapidated and I am not sure it would have been wise to take her on an 80 mile journey with a weight of over one ton.

We had a good look around the boat, made some notes of things which we needed, then headed back to Auntie Rosaleen's for the night.

We took a trip to the shops for a few things which we might need and planned to get down to the boat fairly early in the morning, so we could get down the Muirtown staircase (series of locks) and out into the sea to catch the tide at 10:30am.

The next morning, the 11th September 2008, we arrived at Muirtown around 9:00am and immediately started to descend the series of locks. This canal is a monument to Thomas Telford who was the architect in charge of building the canal. It really was a huge undertaking in those days when there was no mechanical help, and to think that it is still standing today, almost two hundred years later is testament to the quality of the work, which cost less than one million pounds to complete the full 62 miles long waterway.

There are 4 locks in the staircase at Muirtown and then the swing bridge at the bottom. This takes you into Muirtown basin which is a large harbour and berthing facility. At the sea end of the basin, there is another swing bridge for the railway and another set of locks.

The trains take priority over boats, and we had to wait for a couple of trains to pass before we could have the bridge swung open and pass through into the next set of locks. After passing through the locks, there are two piers which extend well into the Beauly Firth, with the sea locks at the end. I believe these were particularly difficult to build when the canal was constructed as there were high silt build up all along this stretch of coast, which necessitated the need for these two long piers to go well out into the firth. The sea locks are the main administrative points for the canal, and the lock keeper wanted to see our licence. I had assumed that as the boat was in the canal, we would be OK to take it out, but a sixty pound fee later, I discovered that I had assumed wrongly, and it was quite an expensive two hour journey down to the sea.

We finally made it into the open sea around midday, and motored out into the middle of the firth before putting up the sails. We hadn't even looked at the sails the previous day, and this was our first opportunity to assess them. I guess you would say that was a little silly, but then we weren't quite sure what we were looking for and we were in a bit of a hurry. The forward genoa looked to be in pretty good shape, but the main sail looked like it could have been part of the original kit for the boat and had certainly seen better days.

There wasn't a whole lot of wind and we had up all our sail and were moving quite slowly down the firth. We passed under the Kessock Bridge and were fairly happy with our purchase and enjoying the pleasant sail down the firth. We were so busy looking at different things on the boat, discussing, planning and debating what repairs and improvements were needed, that we didn't see the squall approaching from behind us until it hit us, and the boat suddenly broached, and hauled her head to the wind.

We both got a bit of a scare, but Andrew, especially, almost dirtied his pants. I have never asked Andrew, but I am sure he would tell me that this was the moment he decided that maybe sailing wasn't for him. Once we composed ourselves, we looked up at the sails and the mainsail was split right along one of the joins in the canvas. We had no alternative but to take the sail down and continue with just the genoa. The genoa was a big sail, and as the wind was on the quarter, she sailed pretty good with just the genoa up.

We went further down the firth and dropped the anchor off Ardersier so that we could assess the situation. Andrew was clearly shaken and I just could not talk him into putting the sail back up. He was used to small boats, as he had owned one since he was about ten years old, and had also gone to sea with his Granddad, pulling lobster pots and fishing for mackerel, but this was a different kettle of fish altogether, and he didn't like it.

Andrew suggested that the best option was to motor round to Nairn, leave the boat there and come back for it another day. I really wasn't keen on leaving the boat in Nairn, and I countered that I drop him off in Nairn and take the boat home myself. This he shook his head at and reluctantly agreed to, just the same as I reluctantly agreed to motor round to Nairn instead of using the sails.

We motored through the narrows between Fort George and Channonry point, where a strong tide runs, and extra care and attention is required to the times of the tides. This is the reason we wanted to exit the canal at 10:30am so that we could catch the ebb tide for going through these narrows. We still had two hours of tide, so had no problems going through the narrows, then taking the inside shallow channel around the sandbank which lies outside the firth.

Taking the south channel means keeping pretty close to the land and it was very interesting to see a new perspective of this area which I had not seen before. It was especially interesting to view Fort George and to realise how vitally important this strong fort had been in days when a naval presence was essential to the defence of the land. In the days when the main mode of transport was by sea, it was obvious how important and dominant a position like this would have been.

Further round there was the more recent development of Ardersier yard where they built many of the early North Sea platforms, but now sadly lying disused. There has been much talk over the years of reviving the yard, turning it into a marina and such like things, but so far, the yard is still lying dilapidated and unused, which is a shame for such a great deep water facility. Potential developers may have an eye on the conversion to a marina of a similar facility at Portavadie, on the Clyde, which has been less than successful, in my mind, due to its remote location.

From Channonry point to Nairn, indeed, all the way to Burghead, there are miles of sandy beaches which would be worth a fortune to the local economy if we could only get the weather which the Mediterranean enjoys. There wasn't much to see as we motored along these lovely, but empty beaches, the eight or nine miles to Nairn, but again it was very interesting to see a perspective on a an area I had seen plenty of, but which now look so different..

I went in as far as the nearest ladder at Nairn and Andrew happily scrambled up onto the pier, delighted to be back on dry land. I cast off and turned her head back to sea without any delay. Andrew spoke to a few older guys on the pier, and they were shaking their heads that I was going back out in this terrible weather. They obviously hadn't gone to sea with the "Swackies", and in my mind in wasn't all that bad a day. I would have estimated it as a force four or five, and I was to take this little boat out in worse, during my ownership of her.

As I was leaving the pier, the engine cut out, and rather than fiddle around with it, I simply rolled out the genoa and was off again. According to the log, I was making around five knots, which was fairly good progress. I kept fairly close to the land again, and noted the sandbanks which lay all along this coast. It was interesting to see the different objects which I had studied on the chart and in the pilot book, possible anchorages, inlets, sandbanks to avoid and landmarks. Things always look so different in reality to what you imagine them, having noted them on a chart.

Once I passed the entrance to Findhorn Bay, there is a long sweeping sandy beach all the way to Burghead, so I set off to cut across this bay, rather than hug the land, which would save me an hour on my journey. Being on my own, I realised that I could not keep going all night, and so began to contemplate where I would take a rest. I knew that Burghead was a fairly decent harbour, but the next suitable place where I could enter at any tide would be Lossiemouth. I decided that I would go into Burghead and take a sleep, before continuing the next day. With a little more experience under my belt, I would have kept going, but I had yet to learn a few important lessons of sailing.

I went into Burghead around 7:00pm, had something to eat and went to bed about 8:00pm. I awoke at 1:00am and got underway again. I sailed out of Burghead and cleared the rocks round the corner and sailed under the cliffs along to Hopeman. At around 3:00am, off of Hopeman, unfortunately, the wind died and I was making very little headway, and so I reluctantly started the engine to help me out.

This is when I began to consider the petrol we had already used when motoring round to Nairn, when we could have been sailing. I knew that I would need more petrol, but the question was where would

I get it? I could go into Lossiemouth, but there would be nowhere open at 4:00am, and I wasn't quite sure where the petrol station was in Lossiemouth. I knew there was a petrol station right at the harbour in Buckie, so decided that I would be best to head for Buckie, rather than wait around for 4 hours in Lossiemouth.

I was midway between Lossiemouth and Buckie when the engine spluttered and died from lack of fuel, so it was back to the sails, and with very little wind, I finally struggled into Buckie at 1:00pm. It is always difficult coming into a harbour under sail power only, although I have done it a number of times. It is OK until you enter into the harbour, then you generally lose any little wind there is, due to the height of the piers.

I managed to get alongside the first pier end where there were a number of people ready to take a rope and help me out. The harbourmaster was there and was none too pleased at me as I didn't have a VHF radio, and he had been trying to contact me. He urged me to go to the chandlers and purchase a handheld radio, which I declined to do, much to his frustration. I simply filled up my petrol canisters and left Buckie under power, bound for Gamrie.

The wind had now risen again, but as it was from the South East, I had to continue to use the engine to get home. It had been a long day, so I didn't want any further delay, and sailed straight across Banff bay with my stem pointed straight at Mhor head. It was starting to get a little rough now, although the wind was no stronger than the previous day, the direction meant that I was being splashed with spray from time to time as Lady Too dug in her head to the seas gathering on her starboard bow. I finally entered into Gamrie harbour at 6:00pm, and Andrew was waiting there to help me moor up.

I remember the date well, as it was to be a crucial turning point in my life. It was the 12th September 2008 and when Andrew came down the pier, he remarked to me that a travel company called XL Leisure had gone into administration. My blood ran cold. XL Leisure was the parent company of Travel City Direct, whom we supplied accommodation to in Florida through a USA company called Welcome USA. Welcome USA had become ever slower at paying their bills over the summer, and currently owed us quite a bit of money.

It was late in the season, and I only had one or two sails before taking the boat out for the winter. I had a few sails, mostly with my neighbour Ian alongside, and he gave me some good pointers about sailing. He did have to tow me in one Saturday afternoon when I had problems with the engine. Pearl was none too pleased as we were supposed to be going to Aberdeen that night and as I was late, she had already left and gone without me.

16

Summer 2009

After the business took a huge turn for the worse, I had no alternative but to go back offshore to work to make ends meet. I was working adhoc, so had no regular schedule and time at home was taken up looking after a business which was still fairly busy, but firmly in a negative cash flow. The business was to take up a lot of my time and it was really good the few hours I could get to go for a sail and get away from it all into peace and tranquillity.

We were fairly late in putting the boat into the water as Andrew had begun a few jobs, which he never seemed to have time to finish. It was mid-June before we got the boat into the water, and I was away from the 10th July until the end of September with only 2 days at home. The bottom line was that there was very little sailing done in 2009.

I had a few day sails and it was more experimenting with the boat than anything else. The first time I tried to put the cruising chute up, it was a brisk wind and I got a little bit of a scare when the wind took hold of the chute and the boat started to charge away before the wind, even before I managed to secure the sail. In the end, I let the main line go, let the chute fall into the water and I retrieved it by the tacking lines.

On another day, I had a fantastic sail right up to Whitehills, but when I turned to come home, the wind had freshened and I had stiff bounce across Banff bay all the way to Gamrie. On the plus side, I learned that this was a very capable boat, even though she was only 20 feet long.

17

Summer 2010

Summer 2010 was the opposite from 2009. I had been fairly busy with work all winter, but at the end of May, the work dried up and I had only five weeks work between the end of May and the following February. This was very stressful, and again it was really good to escape for a few hours from it. Although I had loads of time at home, I was always waiting for a shout for a job, so was not really clear to go away for any length of time.

I did get away one weekend with Johnny, my cousin's husband and good friend, and we had a really good sail up to Lossiemouth on the Friday, with an Easterly wind allowing us to make good progress with the cruising chute getting a great airing.

We left Gamrie in light winds at 7:30am and progress was fairly slow at first. We were even becalmed off Mhor head for a half hour before the wind started to pick up again. The wind was variable and unreliable until mid-day, but in the afternoon, settled into a steady Easterly breeze which saw us berth at Lossiemouth at 4:00pm. The afternoon was particularly enjoyable as we were able to raise the cruising chute, have a fairly fast stable sail in very good sunny conditions.

This was the first time I had stayed overnight on the boat, and although there was not a lot of headroom, it was adequate as long as you were only sleeping in it. The lack of a toilet was a problem, especially if you needed to go during the night, but we could live with it for one night.

In the morning, we were up early, went to the bakers to get some fresh rolls for breakfast before setting sail at 8:00am. The wind had continued from the East, which was not what we really wanted. I had been trying to make up my mind whether we would go to Lossiemouth or Wick the previous day, and as the forecast was for South East winds on the Saturday, I opted for Lossiemouth, as it would be an easier sail home.

Unfortunately, the wind on Saturday was mainly from the East North East, so a sail from Wick would have been much better for us. However, we had chosen Lossiemouth and had no option but to cope with the ENE wind as best as we could. It was a case of tacking all day and by 6:00pm we were only midway between Portsoy and Whitehills. We had both had enough of it, so decided to roll away the sails and complete our journey by engine. It was two very tired sailors who finally sailed into Gamrie at around 9:00pm that night.

That was probably the highlight of 2010 and the remainder of the season were day sails, although I did have plenty of them. I would go out for a few hours, maybe as far as Banff, then back, but I was never settled enough to go any further.

18

Summer 2011

By summer 2011, I had the job all sorted out and the business was settling down, even though it was at around 25% of the pre-2008 level of business. I was on a steady 3 weeks on / 3 weeks off rota, and my closest working colleague, Willie Milne, also had a yacht berthed in Whitehills. We had loads of chats over coffee about sailing, and made numerous plans for sailing trips.

We had a number of day sails, separately, and together, but every time we had 3 weeks off, the weather seemed to be majoring from the North, causing an unpleasant swell which curtailed many of our plans.

However, I did start the year with a bang. For my fiftieth birthday, Andrew had given me a week's sailing training, and he would accompany me. Somehow we had just never managed to get this fitted in to our different schedules until late March 2001, when we booked a week with Westbound Adventures, out of Ardrossan, on the Clyde.

We travelled down to Ardrossan on the Sunday night, stayed on the boat, a Sadler 33, overnight, ready to start our training on the Monday morning. I was doing my Coastal Skipper, and Andrew was doing his competent crew member, both RYA approved courses. Monday morning was boat handling in the marina before sailing out into the Clyde in the afternoon.

We sailed out of Ardrossan on Monday afternoon, across to the south end of Bute, where we practiced anchor handling and mooring.

There was not a lot of wind and we did some exercises in chart work, manoeuvring and general seamanship, out in the middle of the firth. At night we dropped anchor on the north side of the Small Cumbrae, not having raised the sails at all.

Tuesday morning was not much better, and we motored most of the way up the east side of Bute, through the Kyles of Bute and finished up, late at night carrying out night exercises into Portavadie and West Tarbert, where we moored up at a pontoon for the night. The next morning we all managed to get a shower and a walk up the road before sailing around 11:00am.

We sailed back up through the Kyles of Bute again, and dropped anchor just under the three maids of Bute on the Wednesday night. On Thursday morning, we pulled anchor and started down the North Channel between Bute and Argyll with very light winds. Andrew was getting a turn at the helm when we were hit by a sudden squall, much the same as he and I had experienced in the Beauly firth, and once again, Andrew just about soiled his under garments when the yacht suddenly broached and pulled right round into the wind.

The wind grew from this point, and if they had been too light earlier in the week, they were going to make up for it now. We sailed south and took hold of a buoy in Kilchattan bay, in the south of Bute while we had lunch. Paul, our instructor, now set a choice out before us. We could sail east and moor up in Largs marina for the night, or we could sail south and lay up in Lamlash bay in Arran.

The difficulty with Largs was that the wind was to go into the south east on Friday meaning we may have a struggle returning back to our starting point in Ardrossan, but it would be an easy run there for Thursday afternoon. Lamlash would be an easy run home on Friday morning, but with a force nine currently raging in the Clyde, it would not be an easy run across to Arran from Bute.

We unanimously agreed to head for Lamlash so that we would have an easier run home the next day. Before casting off, Paul instructed us to change the reefing lines, so that he could make use of an extra deep reef he had in his mainsail. With a deep reef in, and a No.2 genoa up, we headed across the open firth and I was surprised how well the boat handled it. It really does go to show that any size of boat can handle rough weather if it is rigged properly.

After completing some man overboard manoeuvres in Lamlash bay, we hooked up to a mooring buoy for the evening and settled down to dinner and a nice final chat before turning in. There were five us including the instructor, one less than a full compliment. While entering into Lamlash bay, we did have one unscheduled event, a grounding, which just goes to show you, broaches and grounding can happen to even the most experienced and qualified of sailors.

While sailing up into Lamlash bay, we were brought up with a sudden jolt. Immediately Paul started the engine and tried to come astern out of the sand, however the boat just would not budge. We tried moving all our weights around and all sorts of things, but to no avail. Paul then asks us to blow up the dinghy, and I thought we would row out and drop and anchor a little further out to pull us out, but Paul said that was not his idea.

I suddenly had a bad feeling that he wanted to lighten the load on the boat, and I knew who was heaviest there. Paul would obviously have to stay on-board to control the boat, and Sue would have been the lightest, being a female. Andrew, I and the other guy (I forget his name), were instructed to board the dinghy to lighten the load on the boat.

We tied the dinghy alongside the boat. I was on one end; Andrew was on the other end with the other guy in the middle. When the yacht suddenly jumped free, my end of the dinghy surged under the water. I was quick to jump up and move to the middle of the dinghy which meant Andrew's end when down, and he found himself soaked up to his waist before he could move. He just wasn't as fast as his old man.

We passed a pretty unpleasant night at the mooring in Lamlash bay in that forward cabin, with the waves continually slapping off the bows, and didn't get much sleep. As expected, we had an easy run across to Ardrossan in the morning, before finishing up at mid-day and heading for home with our certificates. We had a very enjoyable week and learned a lot into the bargain.

In July, I had been home for almost 3 weeks and not been out once. On my last week, I decided I would go and try to have a sail, even though there was quite a bit of motion in the sea. I rose early on the Friday morning and was up in Banff at 6:00am. A quick look out over the North pier confirmed that it was not a very nice day, and that there was a sizeable swell running. However, I decided that I had to get a sail, so made the boat ready and motored out past the pier head.

I rounded the pier head and turned the boat into the swell, trying to assess whether it was a suitable day to continue and which way would be best to go. After trying a few different directions, I decided that there was just too much swell and that it would not be comfortable enough to enjoy a sail, so turned the boat around and headed back into the harbour. That was 3 weeks at home in July and I didn't manage to get out for a sail at all.

On the few occasions when I did manage to get out for a sail, Pearl joined me once, and Jocelyn joined me another afternoon. One hour was about long enough for both of them, and then they wanted back to dry land.

At the very end of August, almost into September, Willie and I had made great plans for a weekend sail, and for once the weather was favourable. We planned to sail up to Lossiemouth on the Friday, back down to Buckie on the Saturday, then home on the Sunday.

I left Banff harbour around 7:00am and Willie was already leaving Whitehills waiting for me. For the first part of the day, we had a fantastic light breeze from the South and we made great progress west to Cullen bay. My little boat was very good on a broad reach and I was racing ahead of Willie's more modern, broad beamed vessel.

As we crossed the bay at Cullen, the wind died away, and despite waiting for it to return, we had, in the end to start up the engine and motor the remainder of the way. We got into Lossiemouth around 5:00pm and tied up at the visitors berth. It is good to have company, and as it was still a decent day, we cracked open a can of beer and kicked back to enjoy the remaining day.

Willie had a small fridge on his boat, so as soon has he had the shore power connected my bottle of baileys was placed to chill in his fridge for later that night. Willie had his bottle of Bacardi at the ready also. We had the obligatory walk up the road to the chippers, and then we returned to the boat to sit in Willie's cockpit at his alfresco table. It was probably one of the best spells of weather we had seen since May, and it was great to sit and watch the world go by while enjoying a few drinks.

In the morning it was a short walk up to the baker's for a fresh bag of rolls for breakfast. There was absolutely no hurry as we were only taking a short sail across the bay to Buckie this day, so we were around 11:00am before we finally cast off and sailed east.

From the point at Lossiemouth to the headland at Portknockie, there is a long curving coastline with one of Scotland's greatest rivers as its centrepiece. The mighty river Spey leaves a huge deposit of silt which ensures good sandy beaches all the way from Portgordon to Lossiemouth, whereas the Eastern side of the Spey is mostly a rocky coastline.

Rather than head straight across the bay, we decided that it would be more interesting to hug the coastline, as far as possible, and see if there were any points of interest we had missed by cutting across this 20 mile bay in the past. I was able to get much closer to the beach than Willie, as he had a single keel, and I had a twin keel boat. The risks involved with running aground in a twin keel boat are minimal, but on a single keel, you don't even want to risk it.

After sailing east from Lossiemouth, we did pass a few dogs and their owners on the beach, but after the first few miles, it was just mile after mile of unspoilt beach stretching up to the treeline and sand dunes. Continuing east, we passed old unused fortifications from WWII days, West of Kingston, designed to hinder any possible invasion by the Nazis.

On to Kingston where two small children played on the beach with their mum and exchanged a cheery wave with me as I sailed past, approaching the mighty Spey entrance. I have seen the Spey further up river and have seen how strong and angry it can be, but at the mouth, certainly on this day, it was a very gentle and mild river.

Once we were east of the Spey, it wasn't long before the coastline changed from Sand to rock, and the first habitation we come to after Spey Bay was Portgordon, a small Banffshire village at one point, but now enrolled into Moray. Portgordon has its own harbour and at one point would have been a very busy fishing port, as were all the small villages along the Moray Firth coastline. Sadly now, these harbours only hold small lobster boats and pleasure craft.

From Portgordon, it is only a short distance to Buckie, the largest harbour between Fraserburgh and Inverness. Buckie was a very important fishing centre with no less than 3 boat building facilities right up into the 1970s. Only one of these remain and then only on a care and maintenance basis. This leaves Buckie the largest harbour in the North of Scotland which has been deserted by the fishing, yet still not really diversified into any other avenue. There are a few cargo ships come in, small oil tankers, a facility for the wind farms at the Beatrice field, but little else.

The only bright spark for Buckie at the moment is the plan to greatly expand the wind farm facility in the outer Moray Firth, and Buckie does seem well placed to benefit from this development. It is rather surprising that they have not converted one of the 4 large basins into a marina, as there is a definite lack of deep water facilities on this coastline. We tied up alongside an old wooden schooner, rather than tying up alongside the unsuitable piers.

We berthed in Buckie at around 3:00pm in the afternoon and were delighted that once again it was a very pleasant day. There was no shore power facility in Buckie, but Willie's fridge had kept its chill well, and my Baileys was deliciously at the right temperature to enjoy. We had another trek up the road to the chip shop before settling down for the night again at Willie's cockpit table.

The wind farm vessel came in and we exchanged a brief wave with David West, the skipper of the vessel, before he headed home for the night. He was out again, early in the morning and was able to give us a weather update before we left port the next morning. Breakfast was extremely cheap. The previous night we had gone into the local Co-operative store and on the bargain shelf, Willie spotted a bag of 4 rolls reduced to 15p as they were out of date the next day. This was the highlight of Willie's weekend, getting these rolls for 3.75p each.

The wind had strengthened a little, so we put a reef in our sails before leaving Buckie in the morning. Once we got outside the harbour, the wind was not as strong as we had thought, so I dropped my reef and hoisted the full sail. The wind was from the South east, so a close reach was the order of the day and Willie's single keel proved its worth against the compromise of a twin keel boat.

We sailed along nicely until we opened up Cullen bay and then the wind strengthened into a moderate breeze, and I would have been happy to have my reef in now. Unfortunately, on my boat, I had roller reefing, and it was more hassle to reef the sail in than it was to live with it, and occasionally have to dump a little mainsail.

All the way east, there are a series of bays from Cullen, Sandend, Portsoy, Boyne then Banff. When I was under the cliffs, it was a pleasant sail, but in the open bay, I had to continually dump sail as the strength of the wind threatened to pull her head upwind. Willie, having a much easier option to reef his mainsail in from the cockpit, raced ahead of me and was into Whitehills and berthed before I passed round Knock head into Banff bay.

All in all, we had a very enjoyable weekend and it just whetted my appetite for more cruising as I began to plan ahead for 2012. I had one more day planned for 2011, mid-September Saturday was regatta day in Banff. I had never entered the boat into any regattas, so thought it would be a good experience. I persuaded Andrew and my nephew Paul to join me for an exciting racing day.

I dropped Andrew and Paul off at Banff to take the boat round to Whitehills, while I went to Whitehills, where the races were starting, to get the race briefing. Andrew and Paul motored round and by the time the briefing was complete, were ready for me to join them. We motored out into the bay and hoisted our sails waiting for the starting signal.

There had been a little wind in the morning, but there really wasn't much now, and as the starting signal was raised we struggled to get across the starting line and get going. Some of the lighter boats raced ahead, but the heavier boats really struggled to get going, many of them abandoning the race, and going back to the next starting line for the next race.

By this point, we were well and truly last in the race, so decided also that we should retire from this race and try the next one. Only problem with that plan was that the engine decided not to co-operate and we could not get it started, despite trying many different things and having 2 trained engineers on board. In the end, we had to get the race marshals to tow us back to Banff, and we had to retire in disgrace from the entire day's proceedings.

I was due offshore again on the Monday, so had no time to do anything with the engine at this point. When I returned home, and tried to start the engine, it started without any problem. I went out for a sail, and when I had to start it to come back in, it performed perfectly. It was an old engine, so I pondered what I would do with it, decided that as I was a sail boat, the engine was only a secondary means of propellant, and I could live with it.

19

April 2012 Banff to Inverness

All through the winter of 2011/2012 I considered the weather we had had for the summer of 2011 and the hankering I had to get more cruising in during 2012. I decided that I would give up my berth in Banff harbour at the end of March 2012 and take the boat through the Caledonian Canal to the West coast. I secured a mooring at Barcaldine Marine in Loch Creran, just north of Oban, and began to make plans for my 2012 cruising season.

The rough plan was to take the boat round to Oban in April, then I would have a 3 weeks at home in May, 3 weeks at the end of June, then another 3 weeks in August, before sailing the boat back home in September. I hoped that I could get 10-14 days cruising in each of those 3 week periods.

I was due off the rig on the 26th of March and had pencilled in to sail on Thursday 29th for the canal, however, as the time approached, I could see that the weather was not going to be very good towards the end of the week, and indeed, if I didn't get away on the Tuesday, it would most likely be another week before I could get away.

I got home to the house around 8:00pm on the Monday evening and immediately started packing everything I needed for my trip. Fortunately, I had already packed many of my things before I went away, so it didn't take me too long. I was up to Macduff for a haircut on Tuesday morning, then a quick run through Tesco for food, and I left Banff harbour around 1:00pm with a plan to keep going all night and get into Inverness before the westerly winds came up.

There wasn't a whole lot of wind that day, so it was going to have to be the outboard engine all the way, and it did seem to be working Ok for now. I left Banff harbour and motored west across Banff bay and round Knock head. My friend, Willie, also had the mind to use the nice day, and had arranged to have his boat lifted in at Whitehills. As he had his boat lifted in, he watched me motor west on my trip.

Whitehills is another of these older fishing ports with only small creel boats left, but in our north east corner, Whitehills have been very proactive in diversifying into the leisure market. They have a great marina, good facilities and a full committee which take an active interest in running the harbour. It is often referred to as being the friendliest marina in the north.

A few miles west of Whitehills, the engine cut out and would not start again. There wasn't a lot of wind, but there was nothing else for it but to put up the sails and try to head west and see how things went. It was very slow going for the next few hours, then the wind did start to pick up in the evening, but it was not a very helpful wind coming from the West.

As you cannot sail directly up into the wind, I had to choose a side to go, and it seemed best to head out into the North-west which slowly took me away from the land all the time. Sailing close to the wind, I was not covering a lot of ground, and I did not want to go too much onto a broad reach. I also wanted to catch a nap, and to do this I had to tie the helm up to keep the boat on its course. It was easier to do this if I held a course as close to the wind as possible.

I lay down in my bunk, fully clothed and set my alarm to go off every 30 minutes, so that I could check around. I needn't have bothered, as every 10-20 minutes, I would feel the boat go away on the wrong course and had to get up and put it back onto the correct course. After around 6 hours of this, I was north of Buckie, but well off the land. My options were to continue on this course and make landfall around the Dornoch firth, then turn and sail south-west along the land to the Beauly firth, or turn now and head south towards Lossiemouth. Inverness or Lossiemouth were the two places I could get a new engine.

I felt that it was not going to be a pleasant trip heading North-west, so opted to turn south and head for Lossiemouth. The weather was not very nice by this time, and I decided it was time to put on my waterproofs. That was when I discovered my waterproofs were still hanging in the garage at home. I had packed in too much of a hurry and forgotten some vital pieces of equipment. I was to get my first soaking of the trip before I managed to get into Lossiemouth at around 11:00am.

I had absolutely no problem in heading into Lossiemouth, as I was now pretty much on a broad reach. My problem now was actually getting into the harbour, as the wind was blowing right out between the two piers, making it impossible for me to sail in there. In the end, I had to seek the help of a local fisherman to tow me in and I was soon tied up again at the visitors berth.

This was my third visit to Lossiemouth, and one of the main reason s Lossiemouth is so popular with visiting yachts is because of the great facilities and deep water access at all tides. Lossiemouth harbour, as we know it today, was originally built in 1837, and then a second basin was added later in the century. The port had always been a very important trading route for the nearby city of Elgin, and was funded by Elgin traders

It was only after the harbour was built, that it attracted a lot of fishermen from other places to resettle there to benefit from the facilities. Like most other fishing ports, Lossie's fishing days are all but over, but the local harbour committee have very successfully diversified into the leisure yachting market and have been the example for all others to follow on the Moray Firth coastline.

A call to James Watt, the local marine engineer, who came originally from our area, secured me a second hand four stroke, 5HP Mariner outboard which had only been run for around 15 hours, and had been retained only as a back-up engine. However, he was away all day, and would not manage to deliver it to me until the following morning.

By this time, I was pretty hungry and was quick to get across the road to the local café and get some hot food in to me. I then went back to the boat and had an afternoon nap. I had been up most of the night, and also I was still in a strange sleeping pattern, having come off night shift only on the Monday morning. I had another feed at the chip shop in the evening before turning in early around 8:00pm.

I was up bright and breezy in the morning as I tend to do when I am just off night shift, and had another trip up to the bakers for my fresh morning rolls and a trip to the local shop for a few more essential items I had discovered I had forgotten. I then had to wait for my engine arriving at 8:30am, before I could head off again. It was not a very nice day, but I was very eager to be off on my way.

James appeared early, around 8:20am and the engine was fitted and I was ready to go before nine. The locals were all telling me it was not a suitable day to go, but I figured it was not going to get any better over the next few days, and I sure didn't want to be holed up here for the next week waiting on weather. The wind was from the West at the moment, but was due to go into the North in the next couple of days, which would mean a build-up of swell, making it even more uncomfortable.

I motored out of Lossiemouth and headed West at half power. It wasn't long before I had my second soaking and was wishing I had acquired some waterproofs in Lossiemouth. I persevered though and inched my way West past Hopeman and Burghead, into that long sweeping Findhorn bay. I headed across the bay, but did keep a little closer to the land than I did in my previous journey here.

Slowly I made progress and was off Findhorn around 1:00pm when the wind freshened to storm force. I was pretty glad I was close to Findhorn so that I was able pop in there and take refuge. I sailed up the river into the wide lagoon. In the hurry, I did not consult my charts and very quickly went aground on the bank in the middle of the estuary. A very helpful guy, I think from the boatyard, came to my rescue in a rib and towed me free. I then moored to a buoy and got out of my thoroughly soaking wet clothes, into a fresh dry change.

Before the development of Lossiemouth as a harbour, Findhorn was the principal port in the Moray Firth and vessels sailed and traded as far away as the Baltic. Unfortunately, Findhorn has a lot of silt and sand which is continually shifting, and as ships started to get bigger, Findhorn was no longer a viable option. Findhorn also played a part in the Jacobite 1745 uprising when the French brigantine Le Bien Trouvé was briefly trapped by two British 'Men O War', too big to enter the bay, awaited for it in the firth. Fortunately, the French ship managed to slip away on a dark night.

A welcome meal was cooked up on my little stove, but it was too rough, even to go ashore in my dinghy. I whiled away the afternoon on the computer, before turning in for another early night around 7:30pm. I was in a sound sleep when Pearl phoned me about 8:30pm, and then just catching again when Willie phoned me around 9:00pm.

As I lay there settling back into my slumbers, I suddenly became wide awake. It wasn't a noise which awakened me, but rather the lack of noise, I became aware that the wind wasn't howling, and that it had become much quieter outside. I rose and popped my head through the hatch and sure enough, the wind had dropped dramatically. I quickly got dressed and had started my engine, dropped my mooring buoy and was motoring out of Findhorn within 5 minutes, heading for Inverness.

The wind was still from the west, there just wasn't as much of it, but it still meant motoring all the way west. The sea was calmer and at least I was staying dry now. I headed west making fairly good progress and consulted my charts to figure out my options. There is a large sandbank at the entrance to the Beauly firth between Fort George and Channonry point. There is a narrow shallow channel to the South which I took on my westward route three and a half years before, and there is a deeper, open channel to the North.

In the dark, I didn't feel confident enough to take the south channel, especially as the weather would have prevented me having my charts in front of me all the time. I headed for the first port hand marker for the North channel, and I could see that red light in the distance. I kept thinking that I was not too far from rounding that marker, but it was well over an hour after first spotting it, that I manage to clear it to port.

By this time, due to the area, the shallow water, the riptides, etc., a very disagreeable short sharp chop had sprung up and was beginning to make the journey a little unpleasant. It seemed to take as long again to work my way through the channel of lights, before I reached the narrow entrance to the firth.

My petrol tank was getting low also, and I certainly didn't want to run out right in the middle of the narrows, so I hove to and topped up my tank from my spare canisters. It was a little more difficult than usual with the boat rolling quite a lot, trying to hold onto my tank on one hand, my torch in the other and not spill too much of the expensive liquid.

I finally got through the narrow channel and came into a calm area where the sea seemed to flatten out. I sensed that something was not quite right, and on consulting my charts, indeed, I had wandered a little from the channel into a small bay at Fortrose. There were quite a lot of lights around, and the very bright lights at Fort George were particularly disturbing, destroying my night vision. I was quite happy to get past them and into the dark again.

The Beauly firth is noted for being a choppy place and it sure didn't disappoint me. Before I made the two hour passage up under the Kessock Bridge, I had earned myself another saturated set of clothes. I was also tired and cold and all in all, it was not the most enjoyable sail I have had, but I got there. At 3:30, I came alongside the entrance to the canal where I would wait for the lock keepers to arrive at 8:00am.

Unfortunately, there was nowhere suitable to tie up at and I had to go back round to the new Inverness marina, where I tied up, got out of my wet clothes and tumbled into my bed, very weary at 4:00am in the morning of Friday 30th of March. Although I had left Banff early, my original plan had been to be waiting for the canal to open on the Friday morning, so I was pretty much back on track.

It had been a rough few days, and my biggest problem was all the wet clothes I had accumulated. The marina had laundry facilities, but I knew of a better laundry in Inverness, one which also served good food. Everyone should have an "Auntie Rosaleen".

I called Rosaleen and Donald when I got up at 8:30am and got all my gear together ready for them coming down for me. I went up to the marina office to register with David Findlay, the marina manager, previously the manager at Whitehills marina, and before that a fisherman working out of Whitehills. The cost was £15 odd for the night, and if I stayed over that night, I would be charged for 2 nights at the full price. I thought that was a bit steep since I only came in at 4:00am, and had he offered a slight discount to £10 for the second night, the marina would have had an extra £10 in its coffers.

In the canal, the minimum licence is for 7 days, so I figured I was better to put the boat in there and use up my 7 days, rather than pay another £15.00 for a second night in the marina, as I would only be in the canal for three to four days. I planned to go back in the afternoon, enter the canal, take the boat through to Dochgarroch, the last lock before entering Loch Ness, and then go back to Auntie Rosaleen's for a good night's sleep.

20

Through the Caledonian Canal

After a rest and a good dinner, Rosaleen and Donald took me back down to the boat about 2:00pm and I motored round to the sea lock at Clachnaharry, where there was still quite a bit of jabble around the entrance to the canal. As I entered the sea lock, the lock keeper came down to take my rope, but there was so much jabble, I could not take my attention away from the engine controls to throw up a rope to him. He had to go and shut the outer lock gate first, so that the boat would settle down.

I tied up and went up into the canal office to register and pay for my passage through this magnificent masterpiece of Thomas Telford. For my small 6m boat, the 7 day licence was just over £100, which is a very good rate if you are making full use of the 7 days. If you are only 4 nights, then that works out at a slightly more expensive £25 per night, but still a lot better than sailing through the Pentland Firth and round Cape Wrath.

The business concluded I made my way up the outer canal up into the Muirtown basin. From the Muirtown basin there is a swing bridge and then the "Muirtown Staircase", consisting of 4 locks up to the Caley Marin area. The lock keepers are generally very helpful if you are single handed, especially at this time of year, when they are not too busy.

The swing bridges operate restricted openings at peak rush hour periods, so they advised me that I would not be able to pass through the swing bridge at Tomnahurich until 5:30pm, which was also the stopping time in low season for the canal staff. The bridge operator waited to let me through before knocking off for the night, and I was then able to sail the next few miles up to Dochgarroch and moor up there for the night.

Rosaleen and Donald were a little late coming to pick me up, as some yacht had held them up in long queues at the Tomnahurich swing bridge. I wonder who that would have been. I then got back to Rosaleen's house for another good feed and a relaxing night, before heading down Loch Ness in the morning with freshly laundered clothes.

In the morning, after yet another feed from Rosaleen, we headed down to Tesco's to fill up all my petrol containers, ready to take on the world again. We arrived at Dochgarroch around 10:00am, but I had to wait until a large wood carrying coaster passed through on her way to Corpach. The Kanuta was one of the largest vessels able to transit the canal, and I was later to see her loading her cargo on the Isle of Mull, ready for her trip back up through the canal where she offloaded the wood onto 140 Lorries bound for the pulp mill, just east of Inverness.

I was also tentatively thinking of selling the boat and had a prospective purchaser from Brora coming down to take a look at her. I am not sure what he would have thought, as I had so much stuff in her that the entire forward part of the cabin was unusable and stacked high. At any rate, I never heard from him again, so I guess that tells me what he thought about it.

I finally made it through the lock at Dochgarroch and into Loch Ness. For March, it was a fairly pleasant day, and the only downside was that the winds, although from the right direction, were a little light. I goose winged down Loch Ness on a nice sunny morning, but after 3 hours, I had only made it down to Urquhart castle, and I really wanted to make Fort Augustus and get up through the flight there before night.

Had I not been in such a hurry, Urquhart castle would have made a very interesting stop. This part of the Loch has a very rich history stretching back over 1,500 years. The current castle was destroyed by

William of Orange's forces to deny the Jacobites the use of it as a stronghold after their departure. They were very successful in this as the castle has never been rebuilt since.

I started up the engine again and stowed away my sails, making the bottom of the staircase at around 3:30pm, where once again, I held up the traffic at another swing bridge. After I passed through the swing bridge at Fort Augustus, I began my ascent through the 6 locks which are one of the biggest tourist attractions on the canal. Even at this time of year, there were loads of Japanese cameras clicking away as I was moved up the flight where I found the Kanuta waiting on me again.

I moored up at the small pontoon at the top of the flight for the night and went in search of the local watering holes, via the chip shop. The British Legion is very welcoming there and I enjoyed a few drinks with a few of the locals who were very friendly. This was probably the first day of my trip so far which I had been able to remain dry for the entire day.

Although there would always have been some settlement here, Fort Augustus really only came into being when General Wade erected a fort here after the first Jacobite uprising in 1715. It was completed in 1942 and was captured by the Jacobites in 1945, prior to the battle of Culloden, which ended the Jacobite dream.

On Sunday morning, I was up and made myself some porridge and cast off just behind the Kanuta. The last I saw of her for a few hours was as she left the lock at Kytra, and I waited for the next lift to take me ever higher into the canal. The final lift was through the lock at Cullochy which lifted you into Loch Oich, the highest point of the canal passage.

Loch Oich is a small loch with a swing bridge at each end of it. The bridge keepers were fantastic and had the bridge open whenever they saw you coming, allowing you to progress fairly swiftly through the waterways. Loch Oich is a buoyed loch and in a few places there was evidence of boats which had strayed from the channel and come to grief. Loch Oich would not have been deep enough for navigation, but

Telford artificially raised the level of the loch when building the canal, to allow it to be used in the system.

At the southern end of Loch Oich is the "Great Glen Waterpark". I had not visited it, and had no time to stop there now, but I am sure it would be a great attraction for the many rental cruisers which ply these waters. From Loch Oich, you pass the swing bridge into the "Laggan Avenue", a beautiful tree lined tranquil two mile stretch through to the first locks which drop you down, at Lagan.

There was a barge at Laggan converted to a restaurant and pub, but it was too early in the year for it to be open. I passed through Laggan locks and tied up to the pontoon while I heated up some soup for lunch, before pressing on down the long Loch Lochy to Gairlochy and the canal down to Corpach.

It was another pleasant sail down Loch Lochy, even though the wind from the south meant I had to use the engine again. The scenery in this part of the route was breath-taking and I thoroughly enjoyed this day's passage on the first day of April. I reached the south end of the loch at 3:00pm and proceeded down the canal to Banavie after passing through the single set of locks at Gairlochy.

When I reached the top of Neptune's staircase at Banavie, the Kanuta was in the bottom lock, stuck there because the swing bridge had broken and would not open. It was too late in the day to descend the staircase, even if I could, so I tied the boat up, plugged in my electrics to charge everything up and headed down to the locally recommended hotel, the "Lochy" for a feed.

Early on the Monday morning, when the canal staff arrived for work, I was advised that the bridge was still not repaired and that it was expected to take a few hours before they would have it operational. I decided to leave my number with them and head into Fort William for a look around.

I walked into Fort William, not quite realising how far it was, but not being in any hurry, I had plenty of time. I walked through the length of the main street and bought myself a pair of waterproof trousers and a hat. I had a bite to eat and a pint before catching the bus back to Banavie. I was just exiting the bus when the canal staff phoned me to let me know that the repair had been completed and that the bridge was now operational again.

I walked up the hill, past Neptune's staircase, a flight of 8 locks and a swing bridge and began to get the boat ready to go to sea. It takes a fair while to descend these locks and I passed the time chatting to two gentlemen from the North-East who were descending the staircase with me. During the descent, a pair of tourists were watching, one of whom I instantly recognized as John McHattie from Macduff, my home town. After we descended, there was a fishing boat waiting patiently at the bottom to go in the opposite direction. It was as well is wasn't high season, or there would have been very long queues after the bridge had been closed for almost 24 hours.

It was a pleasant motor from Banavie down to Corpach, where I took leave of my companions who were staying there for the night, and I exited the sea lock into Loch Linnhe around 4:00pm.

21

Corpach to Barcaldine, Loch Creran

Once again winds were light, so I motored down Loch Linnhe to the Corran narrows. This is a narrow restricted stretch of water where the tide runs fast. You cannot pass through here against the tide, in the same way you cannot pass Channonry point except with the tide.

The tide was with me, and I passed through the narrows into lower Loch Linnhe, where the wind strengthened considerably from the South. It wasn't too bad and I could have kept going, but having been able to remain dry for the past 3 days, I really did not fancy getting wet now. I turned the boat to port and edged over towards Kentallen Bay where I intended to drop anchor for the night.

I tried twice to get a hold on the anchor, and in the end I picked up a buoy in the bay. I don't like to pick up a buoy, unless it is marked visitor, as that is someone's property, and maybe they would be annoyed if they looked out of their window and saw you moored to their buoy. Needs must though, and I moored up for the night and settled down for a sleep after a simple meal.

Overnight the wind picked up and turned round to the North. I was not quite so sheltered from this direction, and passed a wild night, where the mooring was never far from my mind. In the morning, the day was none better and it was very clear that I would not be going anywhere that day. It was 9:00am the next morning before I was able to cast off and proceed on my journey.

It was definitely at this point where the decision was made to sell the boat. Being caught in a situation where I was trapped in the boat for 36 hours, there was just not enough room. The biggest problem was the height and not being able to stand up and get dressed, I mostly stayed in my sleeping bag all day and the two nights, only putting on my clothes to go check the ropes.

On the Wednesday morning, it was a much better day, and I cast off at 9:00am and headed down lower Loch Linnhe again. As the wind was still from the North, I was able to hoist my sails and have a leisurely passage down the inside of Shuna Island, past Castle Stalker and into Loch Creran where I was going to keep the boat all summer.

Castle Stalker, mentioned above, is one of the best restored castles in Scotland, due to its unique romantic position on a small island, only accessible at extreme low tide, and with difficulty. The present castle was built by the Stuarts in the 1440s and was renovated between 1965 and 1975. The castle remains in private ownership, but is open to the public.

I moored the boat at 11:30am, but still managed to miss the 1:00pm bus to Fort William, and had to wait a further 4 hours for the next one. The transport to Oban from home was less than satisfactory with a bus to Fort William, another bus to Inverness, a train to Keith before Pearl picked me up for a 30 minutes' drive to Gamrie. This was something I would have to consider. A mooring which had better transport links to the North.

22

Barcaldine to Loch Liurbost, Isle of Lewis

Another boat had been in the back of my mind for a while, but truth be told, I was still trying to recover from the financial shock of 2008 and spending money on another boat was not one of Pearl's priorities. Having been trapped in Kentallen Bay for 36 hours in my Vivacity 20 though, was the final straw and whenever I got home, I set about trying to sell the boat and also searching for a new one.

I put the boat up on eBay and set offers quite low, as boats just weren't selling at the moment. There were quite a few folk watching the boat, and one couple from Hopeman, even made the trip down to Oban to take a look at her, while I was offshore. They were fairly excited, but after viewing, came back and said that it was not what they were looking for. Again, they saw it at its worst, packed full of gear.

It did not sell the first time around and I relisted it at the same price. I stipulated in the advert that I wanted to have one last sail during my time off in May, before selling the boat. One young medical student asked if I would incorporate that sail with his need to get the boat home, and also to learn how to sail the boat, and so my final destination for my last sail on Lady Too was destined to be Loch Liurbost in the Isle of Lewis.

To sell the boat so cheap, I had included the old engine, rather than my new one, and I had stripped out all of my extra equipment. When I got home though, James Watt informed me that the old engine was really beyond economic repair. The bearings were rough and these were overheating, causing the engine to shut down after an hour's running, as they expanded. These bearings would need replaced and the cost to do this just was not worth it for an old engine.

I returned to Alastair, the young medical student, who had bought the boat and explained the situation. I gave him 3 options, firstly to pull out of the deal, secondly to pay an extra £400 and get the newer engine, or thirdly to take the boat as it was. He advised me that he would take the boat as it was and that his "Shener" (Granddad in Gaelic) was an engineer and would repair the engine for him.

This did pose another problem in that we would now be sailing to Lewis with an engine which was less than perfect. This was not ideal, but manageable, if I kept the use of the engine for emergencies only, so I decided to go along with it.

I travelled to Oban on the Monday in Andrew's Jeep, so that I would be able to take all my gear home. The trip to Oban included an obligatory visit to Auntie Rosaleen's for lunch in Inverness, of course. I arrived in Oban around 2:30pm and after bringing the boat into the pontoon, from her moorings, I commenced to unload all my gear which was not being sold with the boat into the Jeep.

I had not included the stove in the sale, but as we had to eat on the way there, I left it with the boat, along with a few other essentials, not originally included. I unloaded the new engine and replaced it with the old engine, which was being sold with the boat and then she was finally ready to sail.

Oban, at a population of only just over 8,000, is the largest town between Fort William and the Clyde. Because of its strategically sheltered bay and harbour, it is the starting point for a journey to many of the islands on the west coast of Scotland. In the summertime, the population can swell to over 25,000 as tourists pass through the town. Noticeably, above the town, dominating the skyline is McCaig's Tower, a building which was based on the Roman Colosseum. The elaborate tower was started in 1897, but the owner's death, five years later meant that it was never completed.

Alastair was arriving in Oban around 7:00pm, and we had decided he would leave his car there, so that there was transport ready when we came back off the return ferry, and I would leave the Jeep out at Barcaldine Marine, our mooring place, which was about 12 miles north of Oban. I travelled into Oban a little early and had my usual chip supper while I waited for Alastair to arrive, then it was back to Barcaldine Marine to let Alastair view his vessel.

Alastair was happy enough with it, and so we were clear to set sail for Lewis the following morning. We bedded down for the night and were up fairly early in the morning, casting off from the pontoon around 6:00am. There was a Westerly wind and we were able to sail on a close reach across Loch Crerran and out into Loch Linnhe at a reasonable pace. After exiting Loch Crerran, we sailed down the east side of Lismor to the foot of the Sound of Mull.

When we reached the foot of the Sound of Mull, there was a storm raging down through the sound, making it impossible to sail up there. We turned and ran back up the East side of Lismor to a collection of small Islets where we could drop anchor and wait a little. There was an anchoring place marked on the chart, just to the North of the island closest to Lismor, and so I decided to drop anchor there and we would heat up some soup for lunch while we decided what we would do next.

We dropped the anchor, but not having an engine available to bed it in was not very handy. It did seem to be holding though and we weren't moving, so went below to heat up some Heinz tomato soup. An hour later, as we were eating our soup, I voiced some concern to Alastair that we were not holding our position, and agreed that we would pull the anchor as soon as we were tidied up after lunch.

We barely got tidied up before it became evident that the anchor was no longer holding and that we were now drifting fairly fast. We got the forward genoa out and turned the boat round in an attempt to pull the anchor, but we were now becoming dangerously close to the next island and its rocky westerly face. This was definitely one of those times of emergencies when we needed to start the engine, and to my relief, it started almost first kick.

We were so close that I had to fend the boat off the rocks with my pole, while I ran the engine full astern and pulled us away from the island. It was a very close thing, and certainly taught me a lesson about choosing an anchoring position in the future. I had thought that we would be OK as we were only anchoring there for a short time and would not be going to bed, but I think the clear lesson is, never anchor where the wind can blow you down onto a dangerous shore.

When we finally got the anchor up, it was a real mess of weed, and it took Alastair a little while to get it all cleared while I got the boat to safety. Once clear of the island, I stopped the engine and reverted to wind, which, unfortunately today, there was plenty of. We headed south again, testing the Sound of Mull, kept going across it, and then tried to get up into Loch Speive on the Island of Mull.

We tried to tack up into Loch Speive, but after a few hours, it was obvious we were making little progress. We decided to take a chance on running the engine for a while to help us get up past the narrow part of the loch, where we would then have a better opportunity of manoeuvring under sail. Again the engine started no problem, but this was to be the last time we were to have the engine available to us, and we would have done better to preserve it for an emergency.

In the end, we were unable to get up into Loch Speive and we turned and came down the loch much faster than we had gone up it. We headed north towards the Sound of Mull again where the wind had eased down a little. At around 10:00pm, at the entrance to the Sound, I sent Alastair off to bed and told him I would call him around 2:00am to take over and let me get a rest.

I tacked up the sound and was able to make some progress while the tide was in my favour, however I was fully aware that the tide would be turning around 4:00am and we would then struggle to get anywhere at all. As I had been able to make some progress, I decided that I would head over in the direction of Craignure, where would try to get alongside the pier and tie up for the 6 hours ebb tide.

As I got closer to Craignure, I would lose the wind, making it very difficult to get alongside the pier. At one point, in the dark, I came too close to an out crop of land and went aground on the sandy bottom. This was around 2:00am and I got Alastair up to help me get her off the bottom and back out from the land a little. It would have been no problem at all with an engine, but we could not get it to start, so only had the sails available, and a set of oars.

The oars were handy for reaching down and propelling ourselves like a gondola, while we were in the really shallow water, but once out into the deeper water, we struggled to row against the tide with the weight of the boat. We managed to get the boat back out a little, where we picked up a little more wind, getting further West in the sound, before making another attempt to get into Craignure.

At times we were so tantalizingly close to the pier, it was tempting to jump in and swim ashore with a rope, but we drifted past yet again. I think it was our fourth attempt, and around 4:00am, when we finally managed to catch the ladder at the North end of the pier and get a rope ashore. We pulled the boat around and moored up for the night and went below for a sleep.

I never sleep very well, when there are things on my mind, and so I was up at 8:00am again and up to the local shop for some fresh supplies. After a quick breakfast and a coffee, we were ready again to head out into the sound to catch the flood tide which would help carry us west. The wind, although not so strong, was still coming down the sound from the west, so it was not going to be an easy day up to our target of Tobermory.

All day we tacked back and forth while all sorts of vessels motored up past us. The big Cal Mac ferry headed for Loch Boisdale in Uist, large ore carriers from the quarry at Glensanda, specialized fish farm boats heavily laden heading east to Oban, then conspicuously empty heading west a few hours later, small fishing boats and even many other yachts who had decided to motor rather than try to fight the wind. Further up, we also spied the Kanuta loading wood at a terminal on the North side of Mull.

It was a pleasant enough sail though and we finally entered into Tobermory bay around 6:00pm that evening. The visitors buoys were well inside the bay, but having no engine, we opted to moor well out, where it was easier to get to, and more importantly, easier to get away from in the morning. It did mean a longer row in our little dinghy, but that was unavoidable.

Rowing in the dinghy had also become a little harder, as we had discovered after our little anchoring mishap that we had lost one of our oars. We had searched a little for it, but had been unable to find such a small object in the vast sea. We were down to one paddle, but still managed to row ashore and take advantage of the facilities available in Tobermory.

Thinking about all the ports I had been into, and indeed, even since then, Tobermory has the best facilities for yachts I have seen. The toilets and showers were excellent and we enjoyed a nice hot shower and a change of clothes before checking out the local restaurants for my first decent meal since Auntie Rosaleen's. After a meal and a couple of drinks, we headed back to the boat where we bedded down for the night.

I woke around 5:30am and stuck my head out of the hatch to see what the weather looked like. It was a "mochy" day, as we would say in the North-east, which means it was a damp drizzly wet day. However, the wind had turned round into the South-east, so I wasn't going to waste that and very quickly pulled on my clothes and was up on deck and underway before 6:00am. I told Alastair to go back to sleep and get up when he was fully rested. I was rounding Ardnamurchan point; two and a half hours later, when the hatch finally slid back and he looked out into a miserably wet day.

We had made really good progress out to Ardnamurchan point, the most westerly point on the British mainland, but once we rounded the point, the wind was on our stern and these Bermudan rig sail boats don't perform so well before the wind. At this point, I wished I had brought my cruising chute, but I had quite enough to carry back on the ferry with me, especially the big bulky dinghy, which we just couldn't have managed without.

A couple of hours later, as we headed north-east towards the Sound of Sleat, two undesired events began to unfold. The wind started to drop and the rain began to get heavier. Our plan was to head through the Sound of Sleat to somewhere in the region of Kyle of Lochalsh, or alternatively, if not progressing so well, to head into Mallaig. As the wind had dropped, we were making very slow progress towards Mallaig, and being soaking wet through and through, just wanted to get out of this weather as fast as possible.

We decided to turn and run into Eigg, one of the "Small Islands", and tie up there for the night. We weren't sure what facilities there were there, but just hoped that there would be laundry facilities to dry our clothes. Again as we neared Eigg, the shelter from the land stole all the wind from our sails and we struggled to get alongside. It was very slow, but we did manage at the first attempt, and tied up alongside the pier around 3:00pm.

We were glad to find purpose built visitors facilities at the head of the pier and enjoyed a lovely hot shower and a change of clothes, perhaps not fresh, but at least dry. Unfortunately, there was no laundry facilities and we ended up hanging up our wet clothes in the small shelter at the end of the pier for waiting ferry passengers. With only eighty residents on the island, I don't think it was used very much.

We made our way back up to the visitor's centre where there was a shop and a café, neither of which was currently open. A few of the locals appeared, and being a small place, they had keys to the café, and were able to secure us a few cans of beer. They were very friendly and one resident even insisted in buying us our first drink. Another local, Donna (http://www.donnathepiper.co.uk), appeared with her bagpipes and when another 4 sailors appeared off a fast rib, a party was underway.

I got chatting to the other sailors and discovered I had worked with one of them, Bob Galbriath, 16 years previously, on board the Maersk Vinlander. A bunch of Kayakers wandered in and the party was going well in Eigg. This was most definitely the most hospitable spot I had visited and will certainly be back here again.

The locals eventually disappeared, the four guys from the fast rib, took off for Knoidart where they had booked a table at the "Old Smithy", famous for being the most remote pub on the British Isles. The Kayakers retired to their tents for the night, leaving Alastair and I the only ones who remained, both taking advantage of the decent Wi-Fi connection available here.

There was a huge tidal drop here and when we returned to the boat, it was high and dry in the harbour which was completely dried out. We bedded down for the night and rose around 8:00am in the morning to find out that the rain at least, had stopped, and the wind had freshened up a little from the North. We would have been able to leave at this point, but decided we would wait until the café opened at 10:00am for breakfast, and then catch the next tide at around 3:00pm.

Had we known the menu and quality, we would most likely have gone earlier. We both felt that the choice and quality of the food was disappointing, especially as we were really looking forward to a good feed before we headed off again, not knowing when we would next have a square meal.

The one thing in the favour of this island was the friendliness and helpfulness of the locals, and figuring out that it would be difficult for us to get out of the harbour, due to the northerly winds, one of the locals offered to tow us out into the bay. This was a great help to us and around 3:00pm, we cast off his rope in the bay, and headed through the South entrance to the island's anchorage point, and along the south coast of Eigg.

We crossed over and sailed along the South-coast of Rhum, and as the day was wearing late, decided to turn north into Canna for the night. There was still a fresh breeze blowing from the North and we had to tack a few times to get through the sound between Rhum and Canna. We eventually picked up a buoy, at the second attempt, around 8:30pm and rowed ashore to find out what Canna had to offer.

In short, not a lot. There was only a population of twelve on the island, there was no mobile phone signal, and the only public telephone was currently out of order. We met a fellow sailor at the pier as we pulled our dinghy up, and he pointed out a restaurant to us, about ½ mile away. He did advise us to be quick though, as it closed about 9:00pm

A Dutchman was the proprietor here, and he quickly advised us that we were too late for a meal, but that he would be able gives us soup, sandwiches and a sweet, if we wanted. The quality of the food here was definitely much better than Eigg, but unfortunately for me, it was very upmarket and fancy, which I just don't do, as anyone who knows me will be aware of. I ordered the soup, but couldn't eat it, so settled on the ham sandwiches and an absolutely delicious toffee sweet. Again those who know me will be aware that I rarely turn down a sweet.

It was now Friday night, and we headed back to the boat and turned in for the evening. The morning brought us a decent enough day with the wind still coming from the North, but suitable enough for us heading North-west to round Skye. We dropped the mooring buoy and sailed out of Canna, not a place I would hurry back to, unless I was specifically looking for a sheltered, secure mooring place to ride out a storm, and set a course for the Westerly tip of Skye.

The wind was very favourable and we made very good progress towards Skye and rounded the South-west point around mid-day. As often happens, coming close to the land, changes the wind you get in your sails, and on this occasion, we began to lose the wind and progress was slowed dramatically. We made very slow progress up the West coast of Skye, but it was an absolute cracker of a day and we kicked back and enjoyed the glorious sunshine.

In the early evening, everything just seemed to come together to make it a perfect day. The sea was flat calm and there was no wind, so we weren't moving much, but there was wall to wall sunshine, it was warm and the Dolphins had come out to play. There were a shoal of, must have been around two hundred, dolphins playing with us, and had they been much closer, they would have been inside the boat. Alastair captured the scene in a small movie clip on his iPad.

We decided that whatever way the winds and seas played out, we would keep going all night, while it was decent weather to cross the Minch. The Minches can be very dangerous and when you get a decent chance to cross them, in such a small boat, you take it.

I went below to conjure up some food and we had a most enjoyable meal consisting of tinned Chunky Chicken, marrowfat peas and Smash. It tasted all the better eating alfresco out in the cockpit. A nice Baileys rounded off the meal just perfect.

Alastair had been around boats all his life, but had never sailed before, but by this point in the journey, he had picked up all the important aspects of sailing and was fairly competent to become the owner of this wee boat, which we would be delivering to his home port in less than 24 hours. It was time for me to start handing over the control to him and leave him to make the decisions.

Jointly we decided to set 3 hour watches and keep sailing as best as we could through the night. I would take the first watch, from 9:00pm until midnight, and then Alastair would take over until 3:00am. Progress on my watch was fairly slow, but when I got back up at 3:00am, Alastair had her running nicely on a broad reach, and we were well out across the Little Minch. By the time Alastair came back up at 6:00, we were closing on the Chiants and I handed control over to him for the final time.

His local knowledge guided us safely into Loch Liurbost to the slipway just below the Church of Scotland around 9:30am on the Sunday morning. Those of you from the Western Isles will know that a Sunday is not the day to be doing this type of thing, and so there was a rush to get the boat moored up and away before the kirk folk started to appear. I quickly unloaded all my belongings and left the boat to Alastair and his father who moored it to a buoy out on the bay.

After 5 days at sea, I was looking forward to the famous island hospitality, and could almost taste that big feed that Alastair's family would have waiting for us. That is the way it would have happened with us at home, and I figured that the islanders would still pretty much live that way, so I was more than a little disappointed when I was offered a sandwich and a cup of coffee.

Alastair's dad gave me a lift down to Leverburgh where I could catch the ferry across to Uist. They advised me that as I left the ferry at the other side, a bus would be waiting which would take me all the way down to Loch Boisdale where I could catch the CalMac ferry back to Oban in the morning. When I reached the other side, I was to discover that no bus ran on a Sunday, so there was no way for me to get down to Loch Boisdale unless I could find a taxi.

Fortunately, I was overheard talking to the attendant on the ferry, and a very helpful fish merchant offered to take me down to Loch Boisdale if I didn't mind the smell in his fish van. I hadn't had a shower since leaving Eigg, so I reckoned the fish van couldn't smell any worse than me, and accepted his kind offer.

I arrived in Loch Boisdale and managed to secure the last room at the Loch Boisdale hotel which is right next to the ferry terminal. I ordered some food at the bar, and headed upstairs for a shower and shave while it was being prepared. After a hearty meal and a couple of pints, I retired for the evening before catching the ferry early in the morning, long before the hotel started serving breakfasts.

A very helpful steward watched me approach the gangplank of the ferry on the Monday morning and rushed to help me climb the 20-30 feet up to the entrance to the vessel with my huge load. I had my back pack with all my clothes and my laptop, another waterproof bag with more clothes and of course, my dinghy, which felt like it weighed a ton.

I settled into the boat to enjoy a trip to Oban via Castlebay on the islands of Barra, the southernmost group of islands in the Western Isles. I do love to see new places, and it was good to go via Castlebay, and I have added it to my list of places to visit at some point in my next boat.

After an uneventful trip back to Oban, I again struggled along the pier with my bags, stopping often to rest along the four hundred metre route to the bus stop. It is fortunate that I did not stop for longer periods, as I had no sooner arrived there than the hourly bus came along and I was quick to board and head out to Barcaldine Marine where the bus service terminated.

I unloaded all my bags at the roadside and figured it would be easier to bring the jeep to them rather than lug all my heavy load to the Jeep. I got on my way, headed home to Gamrie, of course, via Auntie Rosaleen's to see how the old folks were doing.

That was the end of "Lady Too" and now the search for a new boat was on. I was in no particular hurry as the following trip at home; we had booked a holiday in another set of islands, but in much warmer climes. Next trip at home, we were off to the Greek islands. Who knows, maybe a boat out there would be a better idea. Pearl doesn't think so!!

Part Three – Punto di Svolta

23

The Educated Search

I had almost 4 years under my belt now as a yacht owner, if the "Lady Too" was grand enough to be called a yacht, and I had pretty much figured out in my mind what I wanted in my next boat. I had had enough of outboard engines and I also really did not like the noise they made, so an inboard diesel engine was a priority.

The new boat had to have decent headroom so that I could at least stand up if I was staying on the boat for a prolonged period, have a proper table to sit down at with my laptop and keep in touch with the world. I also wanted a proper toilet compartment, although I would settle for a chemical toilet. Beyond that, I was fairly open to the boat I would buy, but price did restrict me a little, as I was still not exactly flush with cash.

I had been looking around for a few months, and had pretty much fixed on the Pegasus 800 as a type of boat which answered all my requirements, but was still available at a very reasonable price. The Pegasus 800 and Pegasus 700 had been built by Ridgeway Marine in Lowestoft from 1977 until the 1990s, so would still be around a thirty years old boat. In all reviews the boat was also commented as being spacious and moderately fast, which sounded good to me.

My own boat had gone cheaply, around half of what I had paid for it, but I knew that whatever boat I bought, in the current market, would also be cheap. Boats were a luxury and in the present economic climate, not many people were thinking along those lines. Boats were difficult to sell, and I could take my pick.

I had watched a nice clean example of a Pegasus 800 down in Wales being offered on eBay over the course of a few months with the offer price being reduced from £7,900 down to £6,900. It was a really nice boat, well looked after, and I very nearly went for it. The only thing that put me of was that it had a hank on fore sail instead of roller reefing. To fit roller reefing would cost at least £500.

There was another Pegasus 800 down in Felixstowe which looked like it had been neglected a bit, but was considerably cheaper at £5,750. Well-kept Pegasus 800s had been selling up to £12k prior to the recession and at some point; I guess they would go back to that price. Early on, when I wasn't really ready to buy, before I had delivered the "Lady Too", I had submitted a cheeky offer for this boat of £3,500. It was no surprise when it was turned down, but now that I was ready to buy, I revised that offer up to £4,500 which the owner countered with a price of £5,250 which I agreed to, on the basis I would pick it up on the 1st August.

In the photographs on the broker's website, it was very clear that I would have a lot of work to do on this boat, but given that I wanted to change quite a few things on even the better kept boat, it did make more sense to go for the cheaper boat and then get it up to my requirements with the cash I had saved. The difference between the prices of the two of them was £1,650, which was a fair bit of cash.

I was a little disappointed to see the nice one in Wales being further reduced to £6,200 a few weeks later and thought that perhaps I had just been a little too hasty in tying up this deal. Of course, you may remember away back at the beginning of the book, in my background, I did warn you that I was a little impatient and impetuous.

I had my boat, and the only difference between the two were a good clean, recover the seating and overhaul the engine, so I guess that would pretty much cover the price difference. The one in Felixstowe had a proper toilet, where the one in Wales only had a chemical toilet, so that was a plus.

24

The Purchase and Planning

I had tied up the deal well in advance and was required to place a deposit, part of which would be non-refundable due to the longer time frame in the deal being completed. As I was buying through a broker, it was fairly safe and the broker held the funds until I picked up the boat and was happy with it. There was a bit of paperwork to complete, but all in all it was fairly smooth and working through a broker helped tremendously.

The deal all tied up, the paperwork done; the focus was now on getting the funds in place and planning the pick-up and delivery of the boat home to the North-east of Scotland. Felixstowe was around 440 miles from Gardenstown, so it would be the longest journey I had undertaken to date.

I had a number of things to think about. Firstly, who would come with me, or would I have to sail it home alone. I would have no problem sailing it home alone, but it may just take a little longer, but having three weeks off, that was not a huge problem. Johnny, my cousin Mary-Ann's husband offered to go with me, so that was at least company. Johnny has some health and mobility issues since he had a stroke a few years back, but he never let that stop him trying, and lived life to the full, but due to his restricted mobility, would be limited in his usefulness.

Nearer the time I managed to persuade Douglas Murray, our local retired baker and a good friend to come along. Neither of these two had a lot of experience in sailing, or indeed boats of any type, so the full responsibility would still lie on me with only minimal back up. I also posted a bulletin on the rig and one guy, Scouse Dave agreed to come, however, on the day he was a no show and it was just down to the three of us. That was the crew in place, so now to draw up a plan for the trip.

I booked my train ticket to Felixstowe well in advance and was able to get a ticket for only £45. At this point I still did not know who was coming with me, so was only able to book the one ticket. Later when Douglas agreed to accompany me, he had to pay £70 for the exact same ticket. Johnny also booked a ticket to join the train at Edinburgh, and so our passage to Felixstowe was all organized.

The grand plan was to travel to Felixstowe on Wednesday the 1st August, two days after I got home from the rig. We would arrive there around 6:30pm and the broker would take us to inspect the boat and conclude the final paperwork, if I accepted the boat. It would have to be pretty bad before I did not agree to proceed, given we had all travelled over 400 miles to sail it home.

Other than inspect the boat, we would not do much that night, other than make the boat suitable for bedding down for the night. In the morning, we would clean up and do any work required on the hull, including renaming the boat, before having it launched. I had ordered a new name for the boat online, as I did not fancy keeping the current name of "Passing Wind". Incidentally, the yard people told me his small tender was called "Little Fart".

We had agreed that the yard people would anti-foul the boat before we arrived and after inspection they would launch the boat for us, all within the price paid for the boat. Hopefully we could get the boat launched around midday, but we had plenty of work mapped out for ourselves in getting the boat ready and cleaned up anyway, that the exact timing wasn't important.

We would allow ourselves the entire day on Thursday to get the boat ready and then hopefully sail on the Friday morning tide around 9:00am. The exact stops on our journey would be determined by our progress and the weather, but it was hoped that we could make Hartlepool on the Sunday and stop there overnight. There were pretty good marina facilities there where we could get a wash and even launder our clothes.

From Hartlepool we would take a further two days up to Eyemouth or Dunbar, where Johnny would leave us, as he had a pre-arranged appointment he had to attend. Douglas and I would continue homeward, arriving on Friday the 10th, with possible stops at Arbroath and Peterhead. That was the rough plan, but as you have read over previous chapters, planning is OK, but reality is seldom as straight forward.

In between the planning and the execution, Pearl and I had a holiday booked to Athens, then to Naxos Island. I also had a course to complete for my work. All this time, I am just thinking, I want to get away and pick up my boat. The waiting and expectation was with me at all times, and I would sit and just look at the pictures of the boat on my computer screen saver many times in the day. However, the allotted time did arrive and I finally got off the rig and home late at night on the 29th August.

The next day was a blur, pulling all my bits and pieces together while also trying to sort through and answer 3 weeks of mail. I needed quite a lot of gear with me, quite apart from my normal clothes and sleeping bag. As the winds were mainly going to be from the South, I would need my cruising chute, which I had not sold with the last boat. As far as I knew, this boat only had a forward sail and a mainsail. I would also need my toolkit with me, as I may have some repairs to make enroute. A couple of empty diesel cans would be essential, as would my waterproofs and my two lifejackets. If there were no more lifejackets on the boat, then I would have to buy a third one.

As we were travelling fairly early in the morning of the first, we agreed to go through to Aberdeen and stay the night with Andrew and Natalie and Andrew would take us to the station first thing in the morning. All this went according to plan and we were finally on our way to Felixstowe. Talking to Johnny, it transpired he had booked the wrong train, and the train he had booked from Edinburgh was an hour later than when our one passed through. No big problem though, as we had an hour to wait in York, so we would meet up then and be on the same connection.

Douglas and I managed to grab some dinner at York while we waited, and we met up with Johnny and all got onto the same train heading south again. We had two more scheduled changes, one at Peterborough and another, with a half hour wait at Ipswich. Since the broker stayed in Ipswich, he agreed to pick us up there, saving us the final leg of our train journey. There was a small delay on the train from Peterborough, but nothing major, and we duly arrived and met the broker at Ipswich only a little late. We filled up his people carrier to the brim with our entire luggage and headed for Felixstowe to view the boat.

The boat was in a yard in an area which was actually called "Felixstowe Ferry", or by some, "Old Felixstowe", which was situated two miles to the north of the main town, close to the mouth of the river Deben. There were a lot of boats here and a number of small sheds sold their produce to tourists and locals who seemed to be plentiful. There were also a number of small eating places around, and that would be very helpful for us.

When we arrived, the yard was closed and the gate was barred to motor traffic. We left the car at the gate and went to inspect the boat. Externally it was pretty much as I expected, needing a lot of work, but nothing I couldn't handle, or pay someone to handle. Inside was a little different, and although I did not expect five star luxuries, I was rather appalled at the filthy mess the boat had been allowed to get into. There was no way we would manage to stay there that night, and indeed, everything in the boat would have to be thrown out, as it was just filthy.

I accepted the boat and got the final paperwork sorted out. It appeared that it was the yard that owned the boat, and I can only assume that they fell heir to it due to the current economic downturn and just wanted to get rid of it. They certainly were making no effort to present the boat in a good way, it was just lying there deteriorating and being neglected.

Now we had to get somewhere to stay the night, and the broker dropped us off back in the centre of the town before we parted company. We tried a number of hotels and guest houses before we were able to secure rooms for the night. Some had one room available, but as there were three of us, which was no good to us. Finally we found one along the front with one single and one twin, and we settled for that, Douglas taking the single and Johnny and I sharing the twin room.

After settling in and freshening up, we headed out for a meal. We found a local sit down chip shop and had a passable meal, although nothing special. We returned to our hotel, had a quick drink, and then off to bed, agreeing to meet for breakfast around 7:30, before going to Morrison's superstore to buy everything we needed for the boat. We had left everything except our clothes on the boat, so did not have so much luggage now.

As it transpired we were up at Morrison's around 8:30am, only to find that it did not open until 9:00am, which we though very strange for a major supermarket. The taxi had dropped us off and we had no option but to wait until the store opened. In addition to food supplies, we bought plates, cups, cutlery, pots and pans, cleaning products, plenty of them, dish towels wash cloths, tin openers, ladles, glasses and loads of other things. We bought everything we would need on the boat, as we intended to throw out everything already in the boat at the moment.

It was well after 10:00am when the taxi finally dropped us back at Felixstowe Ferry and we lugged all our purchases up to the boat. The priority was now to get the hull work done so that we could launch the boat. We could start the interior clean up once we were in the water tied up alongside. I removed the old name from the boat and cleaned up the area of the hull where the new name would be going. It was a big area, as I had chosen a longish sort of name, "Punto di Svolta".

The name is Italian and means turning point. After the events of the previous four years, I was looking, and indeed, believed I was at a turning point in my life, hence the name. The past four years had given me a different outlook in life and had forced me to examine the important things in life. I had been so busy over the previous thirty years; I had never followed my dream of owning a yacht. That was now changing, and I was coming to realise, more and more, it was now or never, and in another twenty years' time, the opportunity would have passed.

We got the hull all cleaned up, the name added and in general, from the outside she was looking pretty good. We still hadn't done anything inside, but decided that some lunch was in order first. We had discovered that once launched, we would have to go onto a buoy as there was no place to come alongside safely in this very fast flowing river. In light of this, it seemed best to have some lunch before we launched the boat and had a more difficult route to the hotel.

We had a nice lunch at the Ferry Inn which had a history as a hostelry going back around 400 years. We the proceeded to launch the boat and get it onto a mooring buoy. Once launched and secured to a buoy, I began an initial check of the boat. On opening the engine compartment, I discovered water flooding in through the sea cock from which a hose had obviously been removed and not replaced. Luckily, the sea cock was in good condition and easily shut off until we were able to get a replacement hose.

Once we replaced the hose, we tried to start the engine, but it just would not start. The guy from the yard tried too, but he also could not get it to start. Unfortunately, their engineer was on holiday that week and was not available; however after contacting him, following his advice, and the engine still not starting, he agreed to come out first thing in the morning to get us up and running.

That was a little disappointing, as we had been planning to just get going that evening around 7:00pm and catch the north flood tide, and get half a day ahead of our schedule. Couldn't be helped though, and we settle ourselves to stay the night. We got the boat all cleaned up and made it habitable, and although the yard had given us a tender to get ashore, Johnny and Douglas did not want the hassle of using a tender in this fast flowing river, and we decided just to heat up some soup for our dinner that evening.

25

Felixstowe to Scarborough

We were up and made breakfast long before the engineer appeared at 9:00am, and everything on the boat was ready to go as soon as the engine was fixed. We had topped up the diesel tank and our two spare canisters which would allow us up to 96 hours motoring at cruising speed. As is usually the case, when the engineer appeared, he had the engine running in only 5 minutes, and we wasted no time in saying our goodbyes and motoring down the river Deben.

We had to sail a fair bit extra south just to clear the sand banks at the entrance to the estuary but we were finally out into the open sea and on our way home. On an inspection the previous day, I had actually discovered 5 sails on the boat, not the two I was expecting. The boat had a No.1 Genoa, a No. 2 Genoa, a storm jib, a main sail and another which I have not yet discovered what it is.

I got out the mainsail and rigged it up on the boom, ready to hoist. I also dug out the No.2 genoa, simply because it looked in the best condition, and hanked it on forward. I did not hoist it, as the wind being on our stern, I decide we would make much better progress with the cruising chute. I got out my own cruising chute, hoisted it and then the mainsail, and we began to fly along to the north.

We made fantastic progress that day, and I was really pleased as we sailed up past Lowestoft, where this boat had originally been built, around 5:00pm, a distance of about 35 miles in 7 hours. Along this coast, there weren't many places you could berth and so it was decided that we would keep going all night, heading north, while the going was good. Towards the evening, the wind dropped and shifted round, and so I took down the cruising chute and put up the Genoa. Johnny and Douglas did not have the experience for a night watch, so the night shift was down to me and I would get a rest in the morning, hopefully.

We progressed pretty well and cleared the Norfolk coast around 8:00pm. We were now into the Wash, and it was a bit of open sea across to the Humber area. I sent the guys down below and settled myself into a night watch, wrapped up against the chill of the night. I peered at the compass which was in a terrible filthy mess, and remembered the new compass I had down below and made a mental note to install the new one the next day.

One of the jobs I need to do was to add an inverter to the boat to allow me to charge up my battery based electronics. At this point, I had always used my mobile phone for my charts and GPS, and it worked well enough, but my battery had gone flat on me, and when I went to put in the spare battery, I discovered it was flat too. I was sure I had charged them all up before leaving home, but that was no good now.

The compass was reading 310 degrees and I could see quite a lot of lights away in the distance, so although I could not tell my exact location, I had a fair idea that this was the direction I wanted to head in. I did have the laptop down below which I could use for a backup, but didn't want to disturb the guys sleeping, so kept going towards the lights.

As I neared these lights, they turned out to be a wind farm, and there weren't a whole lot of lights behind them as I would have expected in the Humber estuary. I had never been in this area before, so was not too sure of the layout. There was a headland with the wind farm just off this, so I turned to starboard, along the coastline there, assuming that the open area to the south was the entrance to the Humber.

It was now daylight and Johnny and Douglas appeared on deck. I was getting pretty tired and I left them to generally follow along the coast line, and I would go below for a sleep. I went below around

8:00am and was back up on deck around 10:00am to observe us still sailing along the coastline and in the distance I could see a large headland. This must be Flamborough head, so I was very pleased with the progress we had made.

We came up alongside Flamborough head around lunch time and this is the first time when I began to get the feeling that something wasn't quite right. As we rounded Flamborough head, we ran into some sand banks, and had to make a huge detour out to sea to get clear of them. Of course, I didn't have my electronic charts and GPS, but on the paper chart, although it was in quite a large scale, I just could not reconcile this with what we were seeing.

We kept going and were rounding this headland, although well out to sea. Johnny was at the tiller and I asked him which direction he was going. Of course, the compass was not much use and he estimated we were heading north. A glance at the sun, which was now beginning to come out, confirmed my suspicions that something was not right. It was now 2:30pm and the sun was slightly on our starboard side. Any seaman will pretty quickly figure out that this means we were heading south.

I told Johnny to turn the boat around and head into the North-west until I could figure out what was going on. There appeared to be a large sweeping bay, and away to the North West, more lights appeared as we sailed in that direction at nightfall. Consulting the chart, I figured that these would be some of the towns to the north of Flamborough head and if I get going in that general direction, I would eventually come to Scarborough or Whitby, where we could berth up for the day.

We continued in this general direction, still being plagued with sand banks, so having to keep well out from the land. During this time of sand banks, we must have sucked some sand up into our intakes and the engine overheated and we got an alarm. I shut the engine off as a precaution, and started it up again after a half hour break. This happened a few times, and then at one point, the engine simply refused to start again.

Being so far out from the land, it was difficult to determine what the lights were as it started to come down dark, but I did seem to be near a pretty big place, and coming in fairly close, it did not look like a place I could enter, so I kept going towards more lights I could see in the distance. As I passed this first place, I was treated to a display of fireworks similar to what I had seen at Disneyworld, Florida, so I figured that this was a holiday resort, but still wasn't too sure which one.

All up and down the east coast of England there were holiday resorts and my thinking was that this was Filey and that he lights I could see in the distance would be Scarborough. I sent the guys off to bed again and I kept watch through the night heading towards Scarborough. I passed the next set of lights which weren't much, and kept going trying to figure out in my head what was going on.

As I kept going, I could see quite a lot of lights in the distance and as I came closer it became apparent that this was a major place. Douglas appeared on deck around 4:00am as we were coming ever closer to these lights, which I was pretty certain would be Scarborough. We approached the southern end of these lights and I could see some red and green navigation lights which I headed towards, as these would be an entrance.

As we came closer, it became even stranger and the buildings I saw appearing out of the night looked more like industrial buildings, not quite what I expected of Scarborough. I headed in real close and entered in between a set of navigation lights, but this took me into an enclosed area with a beach at the back, so I quickly turned around and made my way out of here, and had a look at the other side of this wooden pile pier.

At the other side, it appeared to be the entrance to a river, but as it was still dark, and the entrance was not at all clear, I opted to move further north to see what there was there. Heading north, there was even more industry and a little further along, what appeared to be a major river entrance. I was beginning to figure out in my mind that because I had stayed so far out overnight, that I must have missed Scarborough altogether, and this must be river Tees. There were no other rivers in this area.

There were some low lying islands to the north, and I decided to head west and cut inside them. As we sailed west, and as daylight came in, it became apparent, these were not islands, but an outcrop, and I would have to turn round and make my way out of the river channel I had inadvertently entered. By this time, daylight was well in, and I was pretty tired, having only slept two hours the previous night, so I decided I would have to go for a sleep, since Douglas and Johnny were now up.

I pointed out to Johnny were we were heading, and also pointed out the buoyed channel to him. I explained that this was for big ships, and we did not have to stay within the buoys, as long as we stayed fairly close to them. I then went below to have a much needed sleep. I was only down for around half an hour when Johnny called me and told me there was a problem. He said the tide was so strong that the boat would not steer the way he wanted it to. I climbed up on deck to find that we were well on the inside of the buoyed channel and we were aground.

There was a strong tide running, and I turned the boat this way and that, sometimes bumping along, sometimes getting nowhere. I had the guys move from one side of the boat to the other, forward to aft, and it seemed like we were getting nowhere. It would have been much easier if we had had the engine available to us, instead of just sails. In the end it took a full hour to get ourselves out of this potentially dangerous situation, and heading back out of the river again.

It was a lot farther than I thought to get out of this river and it was midday before we eventually rounded the final headland to get us back into the open sea. We started heading north again and were back on track, and I figured that Hartlepool would not be far away now. A little on our head, there were a couple of vessels working, and as we came nearer, one of them, a guard boat called us on VHF channel 16 and asked us to stay clear of the other vessel which was carrying out dredging for Easington refinery.

While I was talking to him, I asked if he could give me a distance to Hartlepool. He asked me to wait a minute and he would take a distance from his plotter. He called back within the minute and told me that it was ninety five miles to Hartlepool. I thought he must have misunderstood me and was giving me the distance to some other place, so I repeated my destination of Hartlepool and queried his answer. He confirmed his distance of ninety five miles. I looked at Johnny and Douglas, and I simply said "Where are we".

This had completely floored me and I could not understand what was going on. The first priority, I had to know where we were, so I went below and fired up the laptop, something which I should have done long before now. After a little searching, I discovered our location, just off Easington, which was on the north side of the Humber. My head was going a hundred miles per hour. That was the Humber we had just come out of, not the Tees. How did this happen? I just could not understand it, and had to think long and hard before I figured it out.

Firstly, when I looked at the compass, two nights previous and seen 310 degrees, it must have been 210 degrees. Because the compass was so dirty and unreadable, I had made a crucial error which cost us a whole day and much more hassle. Steering 210 degrees, I was heading down into the Wash, which was very shallow water everywhere, so this explained all the sand banks. The headland we had seen must have been the north-west corner of Norfolk around Hunstanton. When we turned around and headed north, the place with all the fireworks must have been the Butlins camp at Skegness or some similar place.

From this point, I had been heading in the right direction, but I was simply not where I thought I was and this is where all my confusion came from. Many things which had perplexed me over the past 30 hours now started to make sense. From thinking that we were near to Hartlepool, we were now faced with a 40 mile sail to the Scarborough which was the nearest suitable port for us heading north. There was never a thought about going back into the Humber to berth up in there, as we were just glad to be out of there.

I left Johnny and Douglas sailing north and went back to bed for a sleep again, as I was still very tired and after the excitement and adrenalin wore off, I was becoming very weary. I was down below for two hours again and when I got up, I could see the real Flamborough head in the distance, and was much happier with the progress. We had a meal in the early evening and after this, the wind started to die down, slowing our progress to around two miles per hour.

We decided that we would take turns through the night, and as it was fairly straight forward, the two guys should be OK on their own for a couple of hours each. We decided that we would set two hour watches from 10:00pm through to 4:00pm, giving us each four hours sleep during this period. I took the first watch, followed by Douglas, then lastly Johnny. As there was little wind, progress was pretty slow, but by the time my watch was over, we had well and truly rounded Flamborough head and could see clearly all along the Yorkshire coast, and I could point out to Douglas the lights I believed to be Scarborough and where he should head for.

Douglas was unfamiliar with the night vision and found it a little difficult to deal with the areas of light, and the absolutely pitch black parts in between. It appeared to him that there was something looming up in front of him, and he had to call me not long into his watch to be reassured that there were no obstacles in his way. Johnny had no problems and when he called me at 4:00am, we were very much closer to the lights which I believed to be Scarborough. As usual, when you think you are almost there, the last little bit seems to take for ever, and it was 6:00am before we finally sailed into port and could confirm that we were indeed in Scarborough.

It was not very easy getting in under sail, and we had to tie up in a temporary berth and get the assistance of the harbour master to move later. Once tied up, we quickly found a café above the fish market which opened early and served full English Breakfasts. We had a good tuck in before I went in search of an engineer to take a look at our engine. It had been almost three full days since we left Felixstowe, but we had packed a lot into those three days. It was good to be into port and tied up, and Johnny decided he would take his leave of us here, to ensure he made his appointment.

I found an engineer, but he said that he was very busy and would not manage to take a look at our engine that day. This was very disappointing, as it meant we were stuck in Scarborough until he could find the time to look at it and fix it. I found it strange that he was so busy that he was standing in his shop, still dressed in his good clothes, casually chatting with another guy as if he had all the time in the world. However, as he was the only engineer in the place, we had no option but to wait and enjoy this seaside resort.

It was a very busy place, and there were thousands of tourists around the harbour area. There were many boats taking tourists on a fifteen or thirty minute boat trip and they never stopped the entire day. One boat full of tourists stepped ashore and another bunch climbed on board. The second day we were there was a glorious sunny day, and the owners had to lay on an extra boat to cope with the demand.

It was a very good marina, but the facilities definitely let it down. An old building at the end of the pier, well away from the pontoon housed a very poor conversion to a shower and laundry area. The facilities were one of the poorest I had seen anywhere I have been up until now. Despite that, it was good to get a wash, and also to wash and freshen up my clothes.

On the Tuesday morning, the engineer appeared around 9:00am, which seemed to be first thing in the morning for him and after that entire wait, the engine was running in only 5 minutes. It was an airlock in the fuel pump which was causing the problem. Having been in Scarborough for over twenty four hours now, I was keen to get going and head north again, so having let the engine run for five minutes, I shut it down and went in search of the harbour master to pay my dues, so that we could head off.

Despite the poor facilities, Scarborough was probably the most expensive marina I had been in to date at around £23 for the night. I paid my bill and returned to the boat ready to go, only to find that the engine wouldn't start again, and the engineer was off to another project, and didn't seem to be much interested.

In the early afternoon Douglas and I took a walk up the road and I bought a few things. A nice new kettle for the stove; we had been using a pan up to now. I also bought a set of spanners which I needed for the engine and also a computer tablet which I would use for my charts from now on, the bigger screen much better than my small phone screen.

We returned to the boat and I tried to clear the airlock again, but didn't have much success. The engineer finally appeared around 5:00pm and again had the engine going in no time at all. It would appear that Jimmy Joiner hadn't taught me well enough and that I was not much more use around diesel engines than I was with petrol ones.

26

Scarborough to Peterhead

With the engine now fixed, I did not waste any more time, but cast off and sailed from Scarborough around 6:00pm on the Tuesday evening. There was a fresh south westerly breeze and with the sails up, we were moving along nicely. I prepared myself for another all-night session and sent Douglas away to bed around 9:00pm. On the VHF, the coastguard was putting out an alert about a huge fifty feet tree which was floating in the Whitby area, so I was trying to keep my eyes peeled in the dark when I passed Whitby, as my little boat, only half of that size would not like to bump into the tree.

Once passed Whitby, there was a large bay perhaps twenty miles across around the Tees area, so I headed across that bay, well out from the land. The wind had also swung round to the North West and it was better to keep out from the land to get more wind in the sails, rather than too close a reach. I made pretty good progress all night and when Douglas appeared at around 6:00am, we were off Sunderland and still heading north.

As daylight came in, the wind dropped off and we were forced to start up the engine, rather than flop around at only one or two miles an hour. I left Douglas in charge and went below for a much needed sleep. Two hours later I was back up to find ourselves crossing the Tyne and heading north at a fine rate.

It was a pleasant enough day and we continued to plod north around the main headlands until we came to our chosen nightly destination of Amble, a river port protected by a sizable island at the entrance and a rocky foreshore. We were approaching Amble through this channel when the engine picked the worst time to splutter and die.

I used one of our spare tanks to quickly top up the fuel tank, but the engine still would not start. On inspection, there was fuel coming out of a loose bleed screw on top of the oil pump, so I guess that is why the engine died, having pumped all our fuel into the bilges. I tried a number of times, in vain to bleed the pump and get the engine going, but in the end had to sail into Amble under the very light winds there were.

If nothing else, I was truly becoming an expert at entering into ports under only sail power. Unfortunately, by the time we had managed to get berthed up, again aided by a local fisherman, the local firm of engineers had already finished for the day, so we would have to wait until morning to have the engine looked at. I did try again a few times myself, but still could not get it going.

Amble was a very nice marina though. There were plenty of berths and fantastic facilities. We both had a shower and a change of clothes and then headed up the road in search of eating places. We found a small pub which advertised traditional food, although we had to walk quite a bit to get it. We had a main course, but weren't overly impressed with it, and I actually topped it up at a chip shop which we found later on, down near the harbour, which we would have been better to go to at first, if we had only turned the right direction when we exited the marina.

We bedded down early that night and I caught up with my sleep. There was no hurry in the morning as we had to wait for the engineer again to come and look at the engine. While we were waiting, we got all our fuel tanks topped up, as we were lying at the fuel berth anyway, so we would be ready to go once the engine was fixed. The engineer appeared just after 9:00am and after his customary five minutes; we were once again ready to go. Again it was an airlock and I began to wonder why I couldn't manage to get that fixed with my nice new shiny spanners.

We left Amble at 10:00am and headed north again. It was a glorious day, but unfortunately there was not a breath of wind and we had to motor all the way to Peterhead. We left Amble and headed north towards the Farne Islands. As we would be cutting across the huge bight formed by the two mighty Scottish rivers of the Tay and Forth, I decided that we would just stay on the outside of all these islands and head north away from the coastline which was now starting to head in a north westerly direction.

All that day, we edged further away from the land until it was only a distant smudge on the western horizon. As night fell, I could begin to see some lights and watched as lights from the north slowly appeared as we started to come back towards the Scottish coastline again. The very first light I could see, from a long, long way away was the top of the TV mast at Durris, south west of Aberdeen. Slowly other lights appeared and by the time Douglas came on deck at 6:00am, were off Portlethen, on the south side of Aberdeen.

I needed to get a few hours' sleep again, so I left Douglas at the helm and warned him to be very vigilant crossing Aberdeen bay as the area was littered with oil related vessels which anchored up there awaiting their next job, rather than pay expensive harbour dues. All went well though and when I got up a couple of hours later, we were approaching the Ythan estuary, and were well on our way to Peterhead.

We finally docked in Peterhead marina around midday on the Friday and I decided that we would leave the boat there and go home, as while I had been away, Pearl's mum had landed in the hospital and was quite ill. Moira, pearl's sister made some "mince and tatties" for us and after a fine feed, Paul, my nephew gave us a run home to Gamrie, ending a nine day very eventful trip.

27

Winter's work

As I knew when I bought the boat, I would have a whole lot of work to do over the winter, and at this moment, in early October, I am still trying to throw it all around in my head and figure out what gets done first.

I am fairly happy with the outside hull of the boat. It is not very tidy, but I think I can leave that until next year, take the boat ashore and do a proper job of scraping the hull back to the bare boat and have it finished properly. I just wouldn't have time for that this year, so it is best left until next winter.

I do have a number of outside jobs though and I did start the tidying up at the end of September. I took down all the running rigging which was very grubby and took them all home to wash and evaluate if they are Ok or will need replaced. I don't think the boat has been used a lot and the problem is more filth that wear. The sails are the same. I haven't pulled them all out of their bags yet, but at a quick glance I wonder if some of them have ever actually been used, although again they need a good clean up.

I want to fit roller reefing to the head sail as going forward to hank on is not very good when you are single handed. I would also like to fit dodgers, a spray hood and sail cover/stack pack. I have located a business online which makes dodgers and spray hood kits at very reasonable prices, so I will most likely avail myself of these services. They will also provide me with the materials I need to make my own stack pack and lazy jack system. Hopefully Pearl will help me out with this one as she is much better at this than me.

I bought some polish and started by polishing one side of the hull which did bring it up much better. Next trip home at the end of October, hopefully I can get the other side done and also the topsides. All the wood on the boat will need to be taken off, sanded down and varnished, as it doesn't look like it has been done in the past ten years.

I also want to fit a tiller pilot, which will steer the boat rather than me always having to stay at the helm. This will be invaluable to me as it will allow me to go below, make food and check my charts and progress while we are underway. At the moment, if I am single handed, which I would be most of the time, I cannot leave the tiller for 5 seconds, and the boat would be off in another direction.

On the inside, I have a few essential jobs, but most are just for my comfort. This boat was designed to have a sealed cabin compartment, but someone saw fit to drill a hole in the floor of the cabin, and the contents of the bilge have come up and made a terrible diesel smell which has gone through the entire boat. I have now blocked up this hole, but I think there are other areas which the seal of the cabin needs to be checked and confirmed.

The upholstery was particularly stinking, and when I got them home to my garage, I wasted no time in cutting the cloth off and putting it in the skip. I will have to try and clean up and de-stink the foam before recovering it ready for the new season. I want to shelf off the forward cabin for storage space, as I will never use that for sleeping in. At the moment the boat has seven berths if you count the forward cabin, but I will reduce that to four or even three berths.

The biggest change inside, and I am still not sure if I will proceed with it, is that I would like to dispense with the quarter berth on the starboard side and make it into a locker accessed from the cockpit. This would give me much more locker space on deck and I would lose a space inside which isn't much use anyway. This would also allow me to fit a fixed proper galley rather than a slide away one.

The other major tasks I have in mind is a complete rewire of the boat and an overhaul of my engine. As you have seen, engines are not my department, so I will contract that out to an expert, but I hope that I will be able to rewire the boat myself.

All in all, it is a fair winter's work list, so if you have any spare time, feel free to offer.

Part Four – A look ahead to Sail with Jim 2013

I have secured a permanent berth in Peterhead and at the moment, I think I will take the boat home here each winter to allow me to get my winter work done, but I have also secured a summer moorings in Broadford bay, in Skye. This should be a better base than Oban, as I can get a train from Keith right to Kyle, with only the one change at Inverness. Once off the train at Kyle, a bus will run through all the villages in Skye and will be timed to match the train arrivals.

I am planning at the moment to take the boat round there in April. The exact timing will depend on my work schedule and time off. The route I will take will depend on the weather. If it is decent weather, I will go across to Wick, through the Pentland Firth and round Cape Wrath, but if the weather is in any way dodgy, I will go through the canal and up through the sound of Mull as I did this year.

Once the boat is round there, I will use Broadford as a base to do some cruising on the west coast of Scotland with my most cherished desire being for a trip to St Kilda and the Flannan Isles. There are a number of other destinations knocking about in this crazy head including Northern Ireland, the western isles and many of the small islands between Skye and the Clyde.

There are many places you can sail and cruise on the west coast, and I hope to have much more exciting adventures to tell you about in my second book which should be out around this time next year. If you would like to be part of that adventure, even just for a few days sailing, get in touch with me. I am always happy to have company. I don't like sailing alone, but have to out of necessity.

Of course, I am only talking about 2013 here. Beyond that who knows where I will end up?

28

2021

Well, you have heard the oft-quoted words of Robbie Burns, "*The best laid schemes o' Mice an' Men Gang aft agley*". That was certainly true for me. I had a fantastic year in 2013 but never quite managed the opportunity to fulfil my dream of a trip out to the St Kilda group of Islands. I had a late start in 2014 due to engine trouble, but I eventually put an outboard on the boat and left Peterhead in June. Despite the late start, I had a great summer and visited places as far apart as Stornoway and the Crinan canal. I even went through the infamous Corryvreken channel.

At the end of that year, I had the boat taken ashore in a small boatyard just south of Oban rather than sail her home. I got her painted and re-engined and ready for the 2015 season. That is when my whole world changed. In January 2015, my marriage of 33 years came to an end, and it was a pretty lousy year for me. I lost heart in the boat and ended up selling her for less than half of what I had paid for her.

It took a year to sort myself out, then I met Janice, who is now my new wife. I also picked up a job down in the Congo, West Africa, and we moved to live in Tenerife, where I had the old longing come back. I had to scratch the itch and chartered a 39-foot yacht for a week out of Las Galletas. There were undoubtedly a few more good stories that week, but that is for another time. Safe to say, the Canaries, with WAZ (Wind acceleration zones), is a whole different ball game from the west coast of Scotland. It's not for the faint-hearted and certainly wasn't for Janice.

That old itch is still there, and once I get settled back into the UK and get roots down, I think I will start scanning the for sale pages again.

This marks the end of the book. If you have enjoyed this book, we would ask you to help us.

1. We would be grateful if you could leave a review of the book on Amazon. These reviews are the lifeblood of my business, and without them, I would have no new customers, and I could no longer write books.
2. I would welcome you to contact us through my author website at www.jamesgwhitelaw.com. I can assure you and I am a real person and do not use a pen name. I will answer any questions you have as soon as I am able.
3. Finally, let your friends know that you read my book and enjoyed it on your social media pages.

Thanks for reading the book.

www.ingramcontent.com/pod-product-compliance
Lightning Source LLC
Chambersburg PA
CBHW072055110526
44590CB00018B/3174